WHAT ON EARTH?

The Plants You Have Never Heard Of!

Stewart McPherson

The Don Hanson Foundation Inc
3414 Peachtree Road NE,
Suite 1500, Atlanta,
Georgia, 30326
www.donhansonfoundation.org

WHAT ON EARTH? The Plants You Have Never Heard Of!
ISBN 978-1-913631-07-9

Sincere thanks to Abbie Mitchell and Robert Irving for kindly reviewing, editing, and contributing to this work.

**Printed on Forest Stewardship
Council approved paper**

*Dedicated in memory of my dear friend Andy Smith,
who taught me so much over the years of the world's
most spectacular plants.
Stewart McPherson*

®

MIX
Paper from
responsible sources
FSC® C014138

FSC
www.fsc.org

Special thanks to

The Avangrid Foundation

and

The Don Hanson Foundation

For enabling one copy of this book to be donated to each of 2,500 schools across the United States of America.

FOUNDATION
AVANGRID

Avangrid Renewables | Berkshire Gas | Central Maine Power
CNG | Maine Natural Gas | NYSEG | RG&E | SCG | UI

www.avangrid.com

THE DON HANSON
SCHOOLS
PROGRAM
FOUNDATION

www.donhansonfoundation.org

www.hansonbox.org

CONTENTS

CONTENTS

LIFE ON EARTH

INFINITE DIVERSITY

What is your favorite plant? Perhaps one of the colorful flowers in your garden or local park? Or a cactus growing as a potted plant on a windowsill at home or at school? Or an intricate fern in a local woodland?

Have you ever thought about how many types of plants there are... or how many of those plants you know?

No one really knows precisely how many species of plants exist on Planet Earth because scientists continue to find ever more undescribed plant species in remote parts of the world.

At least 375,000 species of plants have been discovered and are recognized today, although some botanists (the term for scientists who study plants) believe millions more await formal classification.

Organisms have evolved to exploit every conceivable habitat on Earth, and this has driven the almost unbelievable diversity of plant life found across our planet.

This book is all about plant species you might never have heard of, so you may end up choosing a new favorite!

OUR ANCIENT WORLD

Planet Earth is at least 4.5 billion years old. That's 4.5 thousand, thousand, thousand years. Just try to imagine this expanse of time!

The earliest traces of life can be seen in rocks that are approximately 4 billion years old.

Over literally billions of generations, life diversified through natural selection into the immense array of organisms that exist today.

But the plants and animals alive now are just the latest versions in lineages that go back through time. Over millions of years, all species evolve, give rise to new species, or eventually die out.

If you were to list every species that has ever existed on Earth, scientists estimate that 99% would currently be extinct. The dinosaurs are just a few of those hundreds of millions of types of extinct creatures that called Earth home before humans even existed!

DID YOU KNOW?

- Around 2 million known species of organisms live on Earth today (belonging to all six of the groups described on page 10).

- Millions of other organisms are believed to exist on Earth but have not yet been classified or named (mainly microorganisms and invertebrates).

- Up to 200 million species are thought to have evolved and become extinct over the last 4 billion years since life emerged. Imagine that past diversity!

GROUPS OF ORGANISMS

For hundreds of years, certain biologists (known as taxonomists) have tried to understand how all organisms on Earth are related to one another. The system that they developed is known as taxonomy, and it places similar organisms together into groups based on common characteristics.

All organisms alive today can be divided into six main groups, which are known as domains and kingdoms. These six groups comprise bacteria and archaea (which are microscopic single-celled organisms), protists (which includes all algae), fungi, and all plants and animals (which includes most of the larger organisms we see around us).

Each individual type of organism (known as a "species") can be classified by the hierarchy of groupings to which it belongs.

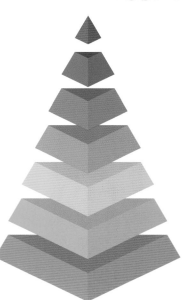

DOMAINS AND KINGDOMS OF ORGANISMS

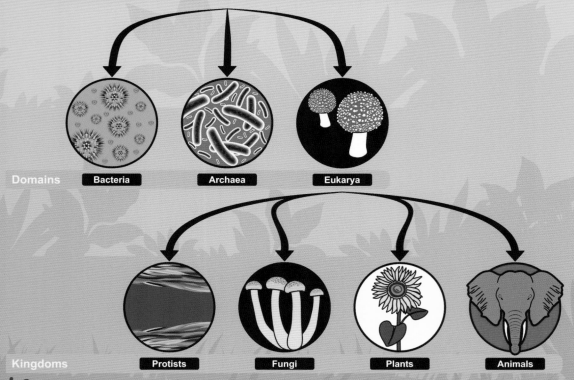

Domains: Bacteria — Archaea — Eukarya

Kingdoms: Protists — Fungi — Plants — Animals

HIERARCHY OF TAXONOMIC CLASSIFICATION

SPECIES
GENUS
FAMILY
ORDER
CLASS
PHYLUM
KINGDOM

BACTERIA

Microscopic, single-celled organisms. Some helpful, some harmful. Among first life forms.

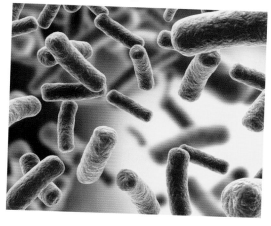

ARCHAEA

Single-celled microorganisms, like bacteria. Lack a nucleus. Can survive without oxygen.

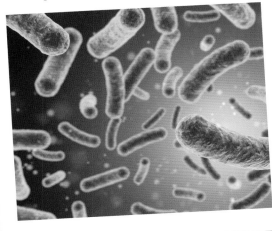

PROTISTS

Diverse collection of organisms. Mostly microscopic. Cells have a nucleus and are highly organized.

FUNGI

Single or multicellular organisms with chitin in their cells. Some live in association with plants.

PLANTS

Multicellular organisms. Most capable of photosynthesis. Possess cell walls with cellulose.

ANIMALS

Multicellular. Consume organic matter, breathe oxygen, able to move, most reproduce sexually.

TYPES OF PLANTS

The 375,000 known species of plants are divided into four main groups:

Green algae are a large grouping of non-vascular plants that grow as single cells, filaments, or colonies. Note: Brown algae (such as giant kelp) are not plants and belong to a grouping called heterokonts.

Seed plants are by far the largest grouping of plants and include five subcategories of vascular species:

1. Cycads (a group of ancient rosetted plants that bear cones similar to conifers).

2. Ginkgo (a single surviving ancient species of tree that is most closely related to cycads. Almost identical trees existed over 170 million years ago, Ginkgo is regarded as a "living fossil").

3. Flowering plants (all plants that reproduce via flowers. This subgroup includes the majority of plant species alive today).

4. Conifers (plants which produce seed-bearing cones, such as pine trees).

5. Gnetophytes (a group of 70 plants that reproduce by producing simple cones, different from conifers and cycads).

Pteridophytes vascular plants that reproduce via spores, including ferns and related groups such as horsetails and clubmosses.

Bryophytes comprise three groups of non-vascular land plants: liverworts, hornworts, and mosses. They do not produce flowers or seeds but reproduce via spores.

Plants have the amazing ability to turn sunlight into energy through the process of photosynthesis. The energy that is produced is stored as sugars, and forms the basis for almost all life on Earth. Without plants, humans and almost all other animals would not be able to exist!

DID YOU KNOW?

- Vascular plants have xylem and phloem (tissues that transfer water and nutrients from the roots to stems and leaves).

- Seed plants are divided into gymnosperms (conifers, cycads, ginkgo, and gnetophytes), which produce "naked seeds", and angiosperms (flowering plants), which produce seeds enclosed in a fruit.

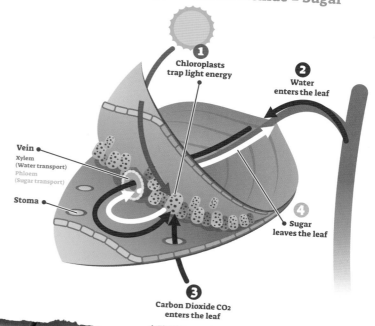

PHOTOSYNTHESIS
Chemical energy + Carbon dioxide = Sugar

1 Chloroplasts trap light energy

2 Water enters the leaf

Vein
Xylem (Water transport)
Phloem (Sugar transport)

Stoma

4 Sugar leaves the leaf

3 Carbon Dioxide CO₂ enters the leaf

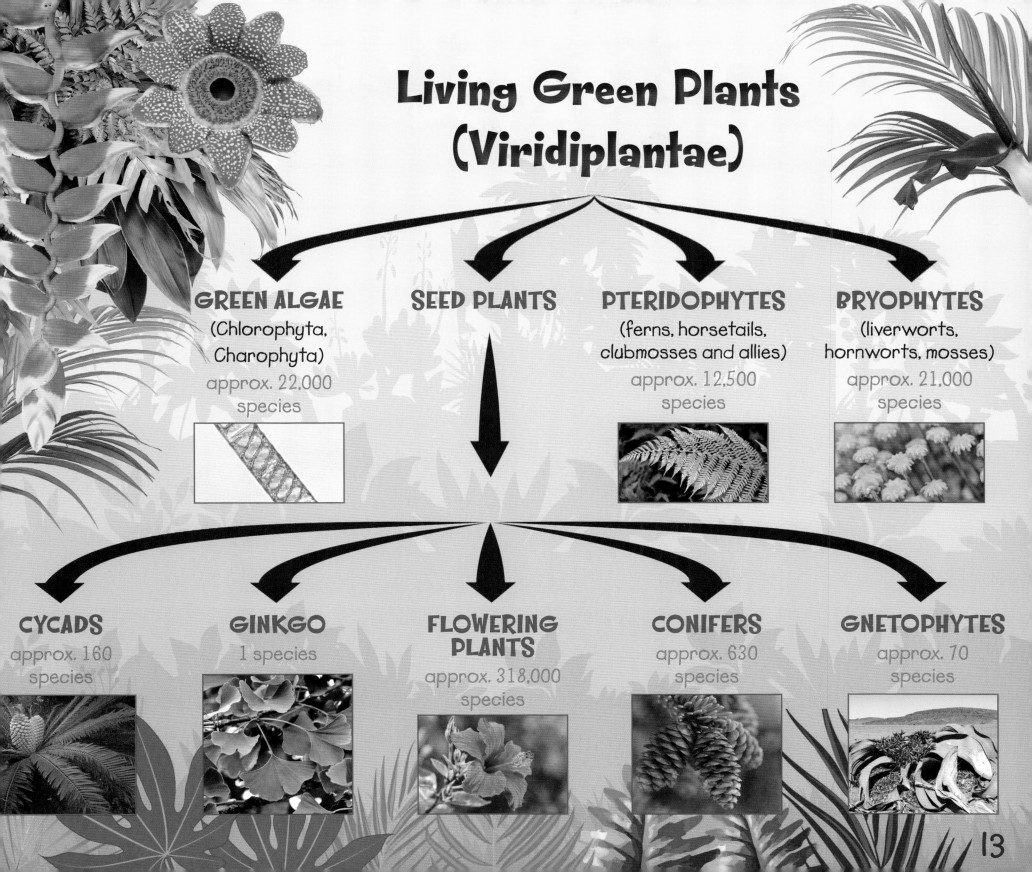

Living Green Plants
(Viridiplantae)

GREEN ALGAE
(Chlorophyta,
Charophyta)
approx. 22,000
species

SEED PLANTS

PTERIDOPHYTES
(ferns, horsetails,
clubmosses and allies)
approx. 12,500
species

BRYOPHYTES
(liverworts,
hornworts, mosses)
approx. 21,000
species

CYCADS
approx. 160
species

GINKGO
1 species

**FLOWERING
PLANTS**
approx. 318,000
species

CONIFERS
approx. 630
species

GNETOPHYTES
approx. 70
species

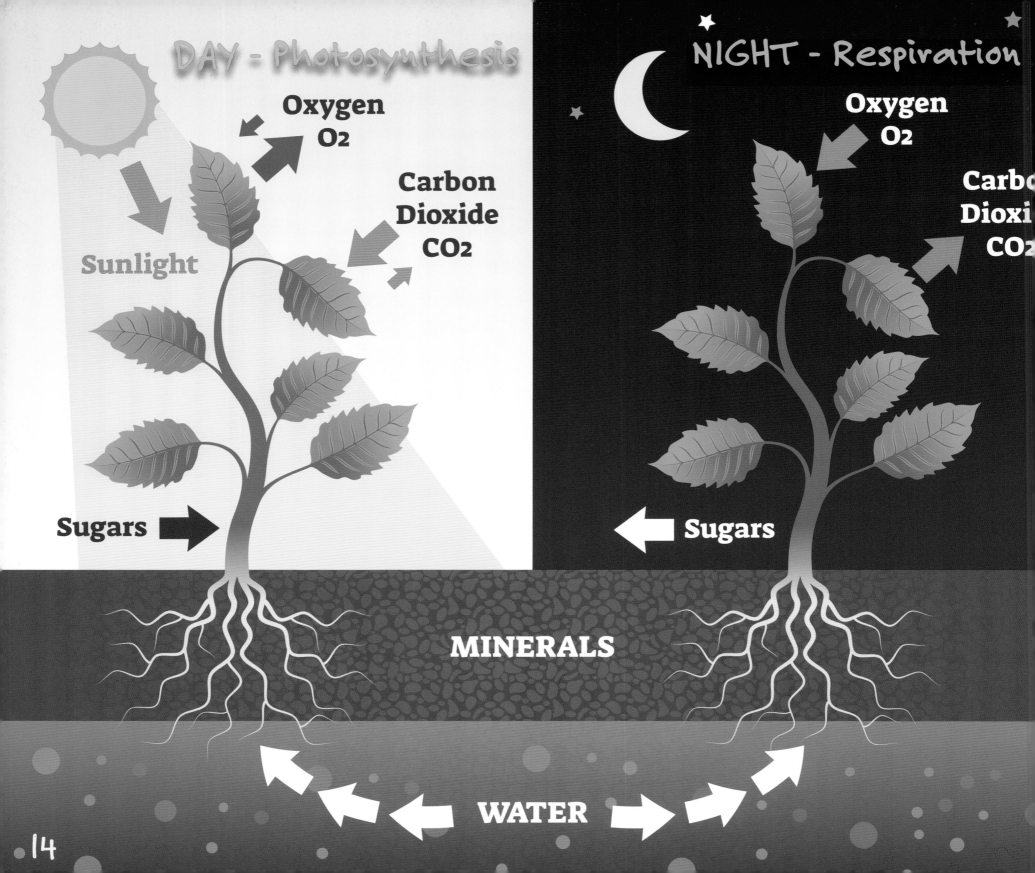

PHOTOSYNTHESIS

Plants use a special green pigment called chlorophyll to photosynthesize. This is stored in structures called chloroplasts in plant cells and is the reason why most plants are green! The chemical equation for photosynthesis is:

$$\text{carbon dioxide} + \text{water} \xrightarrow{\text{sunlight}} \text{glucose} + \text{oxygen}$$

$$6CO_2 + 6H_2O \longrightarrow C_6H_{12}O_6 + 6O_2$$

Respiration

3 Water evaporates from the leaves

2 Water is drawn up the stem to the leaves

1 Roots take up water from the soil

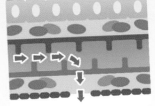

Most plants photosynthesize during the daytime, then respire during the night-time. In addition to creating the food that underpins almost all ecosystems on Earth, plants also generate the oxygen all animals breathe! It is all thanks to photosynthesis, made possible by plant cells.

Plant Cell Structure

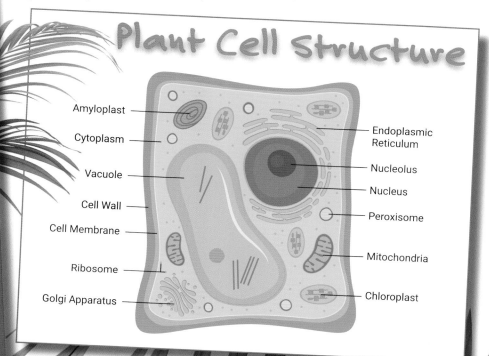

- Amyloplast
- Cytoplasm
- Vacuole
- Cell Wall
- Cell Membrane
- Ribosome
- Golgi Apparatus
- Endoplasmic Reticulum
- Nucleolus
- Nucleus
- Peroxisome
- Mitochondria
- Chloroplast

PLANT PARTS

A plant is comprised of many different parts:

Roots are responsible for anchoring a plant in the ground and absorbing nutrients and water from the soil to enable the plant to grow. In vascular plants, the roots usually connect with xylem and phloem (vein-like tissues which run up the plant's stem and transport nutrients and water to the leaves and other parts).

Stems are support systems and enable the plant to take the form in which it grows. In most vascular plants, the stem contains specialized tissues that transfer nutrients and water to the leaves and flowers.

Leaves are the food factories of a plant. In most species, they have specialized cells containing lots of chlorophyll to maximize photosynthesis!

Shoot tip (growth point) is where the plant's growth emanates from. Some plant species have only one shoot tip, but others can have many.

Flowers are the reproductive parts of (angiosperm) plants. Flowers produce pollen, which is transferred to the stigma of another plant of the same species to achieve fertilization. The ovules in a fertilized flower then transform to become seeds in a fruit. Flowers may be born on long stems called scapes.

Fruits are seed-bearing structures that are formed by angiosperms from the ovary after flowering.

Seeds are an embryonic plant enclosed in a protective outer covering.

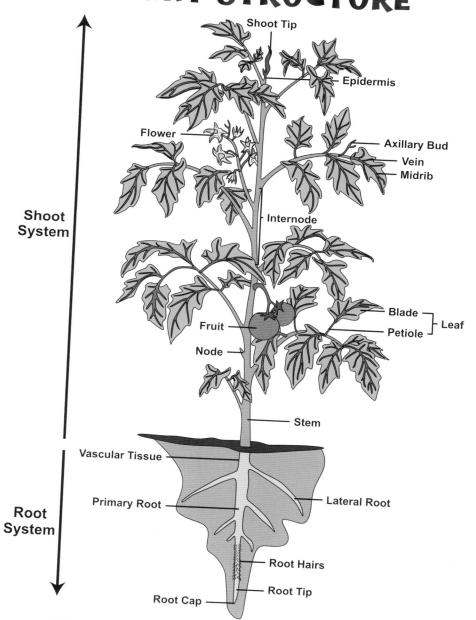

PLANT STRUCTURE

Shoot Tip
Epidermis
Flower
Axillary Bud
Vein
Midrib
Shoot System
Internode
Blade
Leaf
Fruit
Petiole
Node
Stem
Vascular Tissue
Primary Root
Lateral Root
Root System
Root Hairs
Root Tip
Root Cap

FLOWER PARTS

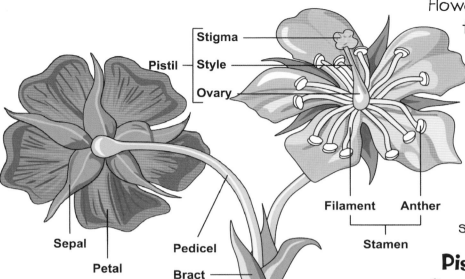

- Stigma
- Pistil — Style
- Ovary
- Sepal
- Petal
- Pedicel
- Bract
- Filament
- Anther
- Stamen

FERN REPRODUCTION

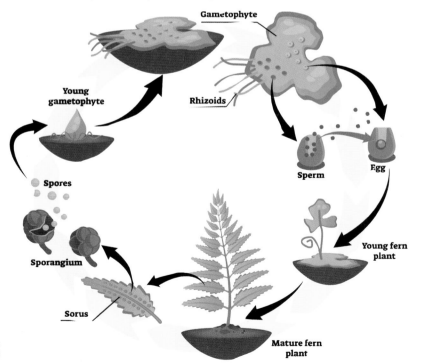

- Gametophyte
- Young gametophyte
- Rhizoids
- Spores
- Sporangium
- Sorus
- Mature fern plant
- Sperm
- Egg
- Young fern plant

Flowers are complex structures that consist of the following:

Stamen are the male reproductive organs that consist of pollen-bearing anthers carried on filaments.

Anthers are sac-like structures that produce and store pollen.

Filaments are the narrow "stalks" that support anthers.

Pistil is the female reproductive organ of a flower. In the flowers of many plant species, there is a single pistil (often in the center of the bloom). It consists of three parts: the stigma, style, and ovary.

Stigma is the receptive tip of the pistil which receives the pollen.

Style is the long, slender "stalk" that connects the stigma to the ovary.

Ovary is the chamber-like structure that contains the ovules (which become seeds, if pollinated).

Not all plants produce flowers (see page 12). Bryophytes and pteridophytes (the best known of which are ferns) develop spores and have a completely different reproductive system than flowering plants. Ferns and other spore-bearing plants evolved much earlier than angiosperms.

BIOMES AND HABITATS

Have you ever wondered why different plants and animals are found in different parts of the world? For example, why are polar bears found only near the icy North Pole, and why are tigers found only in the warmer parts of Asia? How come polar bears and tigers aren't found across the whole world?

The answer is complicated. Many other factors play a role in determining where a particular organism lives, but climate is among the most important reasons.

The term "climate" means the long-term average of weather, particularly temperature, humidity, atmospheric pressure, wind, and precipitation (rainfall).

As the climate of different parts of Earth varies very greatly, so do the communities of organisms (known as "biomes") that can be supported. This is because each biome consists of species that are adapted to the climate present in each place on Earth.

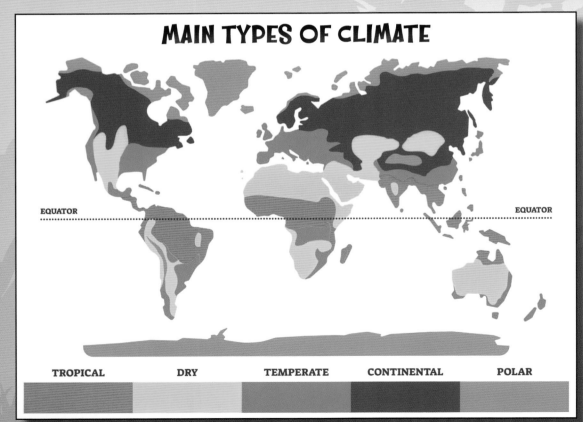

MAIN TYPES OF CLIMATE

EQUATOR

EQUATOR

TROPICAL   DRY   TEMPERATE   CONTINENTAL   POLAR

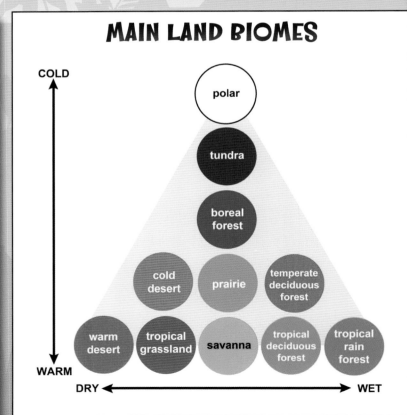

MAIN LAND BIOMES

COLD

polar

tundra

boreal forest

cold desert   prairie   temperate deciduous forest

warm desert   tropical grassland   savanna   tropical deciduous forest   tropical rain forest

WARM

DRY ← → WET

Broadly speaking, there are five main climates on land:

1. tropical (warm all year round)
2. polar (cold all year round)
3. temperate (warm summer and cold winter)
4. continental (hot summer and very cold winter)
5. dry (little rainfall)

Within these five main climate types, the variation of temperature and precipitation creates a wide range of biomes across the surface of Earth, each home to different organisms. With respect to plants, the 11 most important biomes are profiled over the following pages.

TUNDRA

Tundra is the term given to habitats where the ground is nearly always frozen. It's only the top layer that defrosts a little during the summer months. This allows for grasses, mosses, and lichens to grow, but there isn't enough room for tree roots in the non-frozen soil. Below this top layer is the permafrost (soil that never thaws). Hardy vascular plants and small woody scrub make up most plant life.

POLAR

Polar habitats are located at the very north (the Arctic) and the very south (the Antarctic) of the globe. These regions are known as "the poles". Here there are just two seasons: summer and winter. At the peak of summer there are 24 hours of daylight, and during the peak of winter there are 24 hours of darkness. Temperatures can drop to -50°F or lower, so it's a pretty hostile place. Few plants and animals live in polar habitats, and those that do have extreme adaptations (such as the ability to survive subzero conditions).

BOREAL FOREST

"Boreal" means "of the far north" and this type of forest grows in the cold regions of northern Russia, Canada, and Alaska (USA). It consists mainly of coniferous trees and, like all forest, they are important for absorbing carbon dioxide from the atmosphere and acting as a "carbon sink".

COLD DESERT

Cold deserts have hot summers but extremely cold winters. These deserts are found in high, flat areas, called plateaus, or mountainous areas in the middle of continents (lying between the polar regions and the tropics). Like other types of desert, cold deserts get very little rain or snow. However, they may still be dominated by sand. An example of a cold desert is the Gobi Desert in Mongolia.

PRAIRIE

A prairie is a type of open habitat with mostly grasses, but also flowering plants and occasional shrubs or isolated trees. This type of habitat can be found around the world, but it goes by different names, such as "steppes" in Asia. The word "prairie" generally means grasslands in North America.

TEMPERATE DECIDUOUS FOREST

A temperate deciduous forest has four distinct seasons: winter, spring, summer, and autumn. Winters are cold and summers are warm. Typically, they get between 30 and 60 inches of rainfall a year, with rainfall likely at any time. These forests tend to be dominated by deciduous trees which shed their leaves during autumn, regrowing new ones the following spring. Animals also have to adapt to the changing seasons.

WARM DESERT

These deserts are lands of extremes: most of them are among the hottest, the driest, and the sunniest places on Earth. These are what most people think of as being deserts. They tend to be dominated by sand, which can get blown into huge sand dunes. As very little precipitation occurs, these regions are extremely hostile places for any forms of wildlife. Yet highly specialized plants and animals survive here.

TROPICAL GRASSLAND

Tropical grasslands are found where there is not enough rainfall to sustain forest growth, but sufficient to prevent the area becoming a desert. The height of the grasses tends to be governed by the amount of rainfall, and the roots of the grasses may extend 3-6 feet down from the surface. Tropical grasslands are found particularly in Africa and in northern Australia and New Guinea.

SAVANNA

Savanna is a kind of tropical grassland. There are usually a few scattered trees present. Grass cover varies depending on whether it is the rainy or dry season. This is where large herds of grazing animals are found (such as zebra and wildebeest), constantly on the lookout for predators.

TROPICAL DECIDUOUS FOREST

Tropical deciduous forests occur in regions with heavy rainfall for part of the year, followed by a marked dry season. The forests are dense and lush during the wet summers but become a dry landscape during the dry winters when most trees shed their leaves. Shedding their leaves allows trees to conserve water during dry periods.

TROPICAL RAINFOREST

Tropical rainforests provide a hot, moist place to live. They are found on either side of the Earth's equator and receive between 60 and 160 inches of precipitation throughout the year. Tall, broadleaved trees dominate the canopy layer, with lush vegetation beneath. The world's largest tropical rainforests are in South America (the Amazon), Africa, and Southeast Asia.

SEAGRASS

Seagrasses are the only flowering plants which grow in marine environments. There are about 60 species of fully marine seagrasses that grow in shallow, sunlit waters around the world. The name "seagrass" is inspired by the fact that many species have long and narrow leaves, and spread across large underwater "meadows". Seagrasses form rich habitats for a wide range of marine species.

KELP FORESTS

The term "kelp" refers to several very large species of brown seaweed. Kelp forests, which provide shelter for many animal species, are only found in cool coastal waters that are rich in nutrients. Many kelp species lose their fronds (leaves) during the winter months, regrowing them again in the spring.

RIVERS

Rivers represent water on the move, flowing in a single direction. Depending on the local rainfall, the type of ground they flow over, and the stability of their banks, the water may be clear or very silty. Surviving in this habitat, an animal on the riverbed needs to be able to hold on firmly, and one in the water column must be able to swim against the current. The bonus is that there's usually lots of oxygen dissolved in the water (particularly upstream) and food aplenty.

LAKES

Lakes are large, contained bodies of "standing" freshwater, usually having an input of water from rivers or streams and some form of outflow (as well as evaporation). A lake is a fairly stable habitat, particularly in its depths. However, in smaller lakes, oxygen may be in short supply (especially during summer months), and the water can become stagnant. In some parts of the world, lakes and ponds provide a vital source of drinking water for many animals.

PONDS

Ponds are also contained bodies of standing freshwater, but they're just smaller and shallower than lakes. With a smaller volume of water, this means they heat up and cool down faster, which the life living within them has to cope with. Ponds may have a relatively short lifespan, as they can become clogged with sediments and plant growth quite quickly. However, they support a wealth of wildlife too.

MANGROVES

Mangrove trees (of which there are about 65 species) are found in the tropics, typically lining deltas and sheltered estuaries. Mangroves are able to tolerate being inundated by salty seawater every rising tide. They are highly productive, providing a home for thousands of species (many fish use their roots as nursery areas).

MARSHES AND WETLANDS

Marshes will tend to form where land is continually wet. While many plants can't tolerate having their roots permanently wet, others can, and these form a unique wetland habitat which offers food and shelter to a wide range of wildlife, particularly to many bird species.

BRACKISH ESTUARIES

Estuaries form where rivers meet the sea, and thus are a mix of fresh and sea water (referred to as "brackish"). As a result of the silt brought downstream by the rivers, estuaries tend to be extremely muddy places. For birds and fish in particular, this means abundant food in the form of worms and other invertebrates. Consequently, many estuaries have become nature reserves and excellent places to observe wildlife.

DIVERSE HABITATS

Each biome contains countless living spaces (known as "habitats") where plants and animals can survive and thrive.

Rainforests are by far the most diverse biome and support the greatest diversity of species. They cover just 7% of Earth's land area but are home to over half of all terrestrial species!

Primary (undisturbed) rainforest generally consists of four distinct layers (see page 25). But within each of these layers there are countless habitats. For example, in the rainforest canopy, epiphytes (plants that grow on other plants) such as bromeliads grow on the branches of the great trees.

Many micro-habitats can also be identified, such as the pools of water within the leaf rosettes in the center of the bromeliads' foliage, which is a home for frogs and insects!

A bromeliad growing as an epiphyte on the branch of a rainforest tree in South America.

LAYERS OF A RAINFOREST

Emergent layer

- made up of the tallest trees
- sunny
- hot
- home to many animals that can fly or glide

Canopy layer

- close-growing tree branches and leaves
- bright, humid
- home to the greatest number of species

Understory layer

- young trees and shrubs
- low light conditions

Forest Floor

- ground layer
- damp, dark
- home to largest animals

FASCINATING FLOWERS

The 318,000 species of flowering plants produce a seemingly endless variety of blooms that differ in shape, size, and color.

The flower of each plant species has evolved individually to encourage pollination through differing methods and techniques and under the varied conditions of different habitats.

Most flowering plants attract insects and other arthropods as pollinators, but many also rely upon birds, mammals, and reptiles. A minority of flowering plants depend upon the wind for pollination (for example, grasses).

Each of these strategies and partnerships requires flowers of different shapes and forms, and this partly explains why we see such a great diversity of blooms around the world.

regular light   **ultraviolet light**

ULTRAVIOLET PATTERNS

Many invertebrates evolved very different forms of eyesight from ours, and can see ultraviolet and infrared light (which human eyes cannot detect).

Flowers which look to be of a single color to our eyes often have intricate patterns visible only to the eyes of insects.

COLORS, SCENTS, AND BAIT

Many flowers are very colorful, and some have powerful scents which serve as advertisements to pollinators!

Petals specifically evolved for this purpose have as their role to make the flower as alluring as possible.

Lots of flowers also offer bait to entice potential pollinators, such as sweet nectar or edible pollen.

Colors, scents, and bait increase the chance of cross-fertilization because the pollinator that is attracted is more likely to visit another flower in search of more of the same reward. Over millions of years, this process has led many plants to evolve close relationships with particular pollinators, and in some cases, the flowers of certain plant species are only pollinated by a single type of animal.

SHAPES AND SIZE

Flowers vary immensely in size and shape. In some plant species, the flower shape has evolved to be striking, so that the bloom stands out to pollinators (for example, the filaments of a passion flower, shown here).

In other cases, the shape and size of the flower evolved to determine, selectively, which animals may pollinate it.

For example, many heliconia flowers have adapted to be pollinated by hummingbirds. They produce large, robust floral structures with deep nectaries that match the shape of the hummingbird's beak! Having a highly specialized partnership with a particular pollinator can increase the efficiency of pollination and reduce the chance of pollen being wasted!

AMAZING SHAPES

The first recognizable land plants evolved at least 390 million years ago, but the first true flowers did not appear until around 200 million years ago. At around 50 million years ago, many flowering plants had evolved blooms which actively attracted pollinators, enabling pollen to be carried from one plant to another. This may not seem very significant, but it was one of the most important milestones in the evolution of life on Earth.

Suddenly, individual plants could exchange genetic information very efficiently. This led to an explosion of plant types, with millions of new flowering plant species evolving.

Out of the hundreds of thousands of different flowers, some just happen to resemble objects we recognize! Here are some examples.

FLYING DUCK ORCHID

In Australia, the flying duck orchid (*Caleana major*) produces complex duck-shaped blooms that evolved to attract male sawflies!

Despite its similarity to a duck in our eyes, the flower closely resembles the color, size, and shape of female sawflies. The poor males are tricked into thinking the flower is a female, then become laden with pollen!

BEE ORCHIDS (*Ophrys apifera*) produce flowers that closely resemble the furry body, color, and scent of bees!

MONKEY FACE ORCHIDS (*Dracula simia*) from South America produce blooms that seemingly have a mouth, a nose, and two eyes staring out of them!

Many species of NAKED MAN ORCHIDS (*Oncidium* spp.) from Europe and Asia produce flowers that look just like dancing, naked men!

The DANCING GIRL BEGONIA (*Impatiens bequaertii*) is a miniature species of balsam from the rainforests of Africa.

The plants only grow to about 8 inches and produce amazing flowers that are just 0.5 inches long and resemble little girls wearing ballet dresses with their arms outstretched.

The WHITE EGRET ORCHID (*Habenaria radiata* above) produces blooms that look a lot like flying egrets!

The HOT LIPS FLOWER (*Psychotria elata*) produces bright red, puckered lips that look as if they are about to give a smooch! Tiny, star-shaped flowers emerge between them, which attract butterflies and hummingbirds.

LADY'S SLIPPER FLOWERS (*Calceolaria fothergillii*) grow in the Falkland Islands on rocky slopes. They produce blooms that look like slippers, but also resemble a bizarre, gaping face with googly eyes!

SKULL POD SNAPDRAGON (*Antirrhinum majus*) is a popular garden flower, coming in many beautiful varieties. But its seed pods couldn't be more different – they look like moaning skulls with large foreheads! The good news is that they're easy to grow, and will please those who love gruesome-looking things. Like pansies, these tough plants do best outside in a flower bed, pot, or window box. They prefer a sunny spot with damp, freely draining potting mix and temperatures of 50˚–85˚F in summer.

DARTH VADER FLOWER

Some plants produce flowers that look terrifying!

The DARTH VADER FLOWER (*Aristolochia salvadorensis*) is a tropical vine that produces flowers that hang in mid air and resemble the helmets of the evil cyborg ruler from *Star Wars*. The little helmet-shaped flowers even have two pale eye-sockets that stare out at you from the depths of the jungle!

It is thought to be pollinated by (brave!) insects.

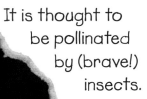

In 2014, the DARTH VADER BEGONIA was discovered on the island of Borneo. Its leaves are so intensely green that they almost appear black, and so it was named *Begonia darthvaderiana* after Darth Vader from the *Star Wars* films.

It grows in deep shade, and the very dark coloration enables its leaves to absorb what little sunlight can pass through the dense layers of the rainforest. If you discover a new species, you can name your discovery after anything or anyone you like (although your name needs to be Latinized)! Hundreds of new species of plants continue to be found every year!

What on Earth? The Plants You Have Never Heard Of!

BIRD OF PARADISE FLOWER

The bird of paradise flower (*Strelitzia reginae*) from South Africa has a really flamboyant flower!

It is so called because of a resemblance of its flowers to the birds of paradise of New Guinea (see photo to the left), although it is pollinated by African sunbirds.

Sunbirds visit the bird of paradise flower, sometimes using the blue stamen as a perch to stand on while licking nectar from its base. The weight of the bird standing on the stamen causes it to split open and release pollen onto the bird's feet. When the bird flies to the next flower, it deposits pollen on the white, sticky stigma located at the tip of the stamen.

Interestingly, the seeds of the bird of paradise have strange tufts of bright orange filaments!

stamen

stigma

seeds

LOBSTER CLAW FLOWERS

Hummingbirds often migrate vast distances across the Americas and need to drink nectar regularly to refuel with energy.

One group of plants called *Heliconia*, from the Americas, have evolved to be hummingbird fueling stations, and have flowers that are adapted perfectly to suit their curved beaks. In many *Heliconia*, the hummingbird is able to perch on a flower and, as it reaches into the nectaries to drink the honey-sweet nectar, the plant deposits a dab of pollen on the top of its head, so the next time it visits a flower, it delivers the pollen!

Some *Heliconia* arrange their flowers in spectacular groups that can hang together in rows and measure 3 feet or more! The flowers of one species look just like red lobster claws!

PASSION FLOWERS

Passion flowers (*Passiflora*) produce some of the most colorful and bizarre flowers in the entire plant kingdom.

There are over 550 species of passion flowers, and they occur in almost every possible combination of colors, often with incredible stripes and patterns.

Most species come from Central and South America, and attract a wide range of pollinators that can include bees, wasps, and beetles, and also bats and hummingbirds too!

Many species produce delicious fruits! Have you ever tried passionfruit ice cream?

BAT FLOWERS

Lurking in the shadows of the tropical rainforest, the black bat flower (*Tacca chantrieri*) is one of the most bizarre flowers of all plants. It originates from Southeast Asia along with several other closely related species.

The flower scape is dark purple, maroon, or black, and consists of two pairs of bat wing-like bracts with thread-like whiskers growing beneath them, known as bracteoles.

Up to 25 small, round flowers emerge on stalks and point upward when they are open, then droop downward when they have finished flowering. The whole structure may be up to 20 inches tall and 12 inches wide.

No one is really sure why the flowers are shaped in the bizarre bat-like way that they are. Some botanists believe that the color and shape of the flowers resemble rotting organic material to attract flies. Others have suggested that the strange shape of the flower evolved to enable self-pollination. A last theory is that the whiskers allow ants to climb up to the flowers and cross-pollinate them.

Nightmare PARASITE!

A group of parasitic plants from Asia called *Rhizanthes* produce perhaps the most grotesque flowers of all plants. *Rhizanthes* blooms look like an exploded octopus spread on the ground. They have many petals, each of which terminates in a tendril that spreads onto the rainforest floor.

The *Rhizanthes* flower stinks of rotting meat and attracts carrion flies to the smelly, brownish, hairy blooms. The deception is so perfect that the flies often lay eggs on the surface of the bloom (thinking it to be a dead animal).

As they explore the flower, the pollen-laden flies fertilize the bloom. The fly eggs frequently hatch, and tiny maggots crawl over the surface of the *Rhizanthes* flower, only to find no meat meal at all. The maggots eventually all die of starvation or are killed by ants, which climb onto the flower by crawling along the strange tentacles. For this reason, one *Rhizanthes* species is called *Rhizanthes infanticida* – the infant (baby fly) killing plant!

POM POMS LANDSCAPE

A vast woody-savanna biome called the Cerrado stretches across tropical and subtropical parts of Brazil.

It is home to a group of spectacular plants that belong to the pipeworts family (*Paepalanthus* spp.). These plants produce very unusual floral structures that are arranged like pom poms.

Each year, millions of blooms open together, creating a landscape of white pom poms! It has been described as one of the most striking displays of flowers on Earth!

FRUIT AND SEEDS

Once a pollen grain lands on the stigma of a flower, it sprouts a tube which grows through the tissue of the style until it reaches the ovary.

The nucleus of the pollen grain (the male gamete) then passes along the pollen tube and joins with the nucleus of the ovule (the female gamete). The flower is then fertilized.

Depending upon the species of plant, the ovary swells and transforms into a fruit, and the ovules develop to become seeds.

The fruit of many plants are adapted to disseminate their seeds by being edible. This encourages animals to eat the fruit, which enables the seeds to be dispersed, resulting in the plant's range being reinforced or expanded.

 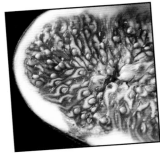 

OLDEST VIABLE SEEDS

Seeds are incredible! They contain an embryonic plant enclosed in a protective outer covering and can dry out or freeze but still remain viable.

Seeds of a plant called *Silene stenophylla* grew after being frozen in permafrost for over 30,000 years! Those of a 1,300 year old sacred lotus (above) found in a dry riverbed also germinated!

FLYING SEEDS

Although many plants produce fruit to encourage animals to disperse their seeds, others produce seeds that can glide! For instance, the dandelion produces little seeds with parachutes that are easily carried by gusts of wind.

Many trees (such as sycamores) produce seeds with "chopper blade" wings that cause the seed to rotate and fly like a helicopter as they fall.

The seeds of the Javan cucumber (*Alsomitra macrocarpa*) are equipped with transparent hang-glider wings that are so efficient that they can glide through the jungle carried by the faintest winds. They have been known to travel miles when blown by the wind and so enable the species to spread into new habitats!

FLOATING SEEDS

A few plants produce seeds that disperse by floating, and chances are you have eaten one – the coconut!

Coconuts are actually seeds. In the wild, they have thick husks which enable them to float! Coconut palms often grow close to water and spread along coasts and to neighboring islands as a result of their floating seeds.

But the very best floating seeds of all belong to the sea bean (*Entada rheedii*). It grows as a vine and produces massive hanging seed pods that can be over 5 feet long! The pods contain large, round, brown seeds that can be up to 5 inches in diameter. These huge beans float very well and can drift on ocean currents for years before washing ashore on distant beaches and germinating.

All of the crop plants which produce the fruit and vegetables that people eat today were originally developed from wild plants, in some cases thousands of years ago.

As civilizations around the world emerged, the first farmers in each area found different groups of edible plants in their local area that they could cultivate to produce delicious vegetables and fruits. Wild plants were selectively bred to create bigger and tastier fruit, in ever greater amounts.

Gradually, this process produced the fruit and vegetables that we know and eat today.

Each region of the world naturally has very different groups of native plants, and the different civilizations came to rely on different crops as their fruit and vegetable staples.

Today, we have access to fruit and vegetables from all corners of the globe, but the types of fruits and vegetables that you see in the supermarket are just a few of the tens of thousands of crop plants that humans have developed across the world over thousands of years.

Many of the fruits and vegetables that we know today are actually just popular examples of really diverse fruits and vegetables that occur in amazing ranges of colors, shapes, and sizes in the regions where they were originally cultivated.

For example, beans aren't just baked, broad, or green. There are thousands of types of beans in all shapes, sizes, and colors.

Purple is quite a widespread color in many wild strains of fruit and vegetables. There are types of cauliflowers, broccoli, and sweet potatoes that are bright purple! Would you eat these bright purple fruit?

Many parts of the world have completely different fruits and vegetables than those we are familiar with. The apples and pears we eat every day are their exotic and expensive rarities! For example, in many parts of tropical Indonesia, temperate fruits can be difficult to find, but bright red bananas and the bizarre-looking snake fruit (the fruit of a palm with scaly brown skin) are the everyday.

In this chapter, we will explore some of the world's most unusual fruits and vegetables. Many of these can be found at specialty shops or grown from seed.

JEWEL CORN

Sweetcorn, also known as maize, was domesticated in Central America from a species of grass around 9,000 years ago! It had been cultivated by indigenous people across the Americas for thousands of years, before it was encountered by European explorers and carried back to Europe some 500 years ago.

Sweetcorn remains the most widely grown crop across the Americas, where it is known as "corn", and, particularly in Central America, it is eaten during almost every meal in one form or another. It has also become an important staple across many other parts of the world.

But over the centuries, hundreds of different strains have been selectively bred which produce an incredible variety of kernels that differ in color, shape, and size. Some breeds of Central American corn were cultivated specifically for producing flour.

Many breeds of Central American corn have fantastic, descriptive names:

"Glass gem" corn produces multicolored, glossy, jewel-like kernels (see photo, left).

"Strawberry" corn produces little ears of tiny red kernels (bottom left).

"Oaxacan green dent" corn produces bright green kernels (above).

But perhaps the most unusual variety of all is black corn (below). This was grown by the Aztecs who worshipped several gods of corn, including Centeotl (the "Corn Cob Lord"), Xilonen (goddess of sweetcorn), and Chicomecoátl (goddess of seed corn). Several figurines have been found with hairstyles resembling ears of corn, and Aztec mythology holds that the god Quetzalcoatl stole a kernel of corn for the humans to plant.

For at least 2,000 years, black Aztec corn has had a particularly important significance for indigenous groups of the Americas. It was (and still is) used to make an alcoholic drink called masato, and features in ancient folklore, ceremonial costumes, and myths.

RAINBOW CARROTS

Carrots are the roots of the wild carrot (*Daucus carota*), a species thought to have originated in the mountains of Afghanistan and Iran, and long since domesticated across Asia and Europe.

We think of carrots as bright orange, skinny taproots, but the orange carrots we know today were actually bred by Dutch growers during the 16th and 17th centuries. Before then, carrots occurred in a rainbow of colors, including purple, red, white, and yellow, and in a variety of shapes, from small, ball-shaped ones to wide, chunky ones! Many of these are still cultivated and are easy to grow at home or in your classroom.

WHITE STRAWBERRIES!

Strawberries are delicious, but there is a little-known relative called the pineberry which is perhaps even tastier!

It is so-called because it tastes just like pineapple and produces little white berries (up to 1 inch across) that are speckled with red seeds (the opposite of normal strawberries).

Pineberries are actually hybrid strawberries involving species from Europe, North America, and Chile, so they do not occur naturally.

Pineberries do not grow true from seed, so you will need to buy young starter plants to grow true pineberries successfully.

BLACK TOMATOES

Believe it or not, tomatoes belong to the nightshade family, which includes many very poisonous relatives! The fruit of wild tomato species often have a very bitter taste, but some are sweeter than others.

They originate in the Andes Mountains of South America, and it is thought that the first tomatoes arrived in Europe from Peru, having been transported home by the Spanish.

Hundreds of strains of tomatoes have been bred, including yellow, orange, pink, and even pure black varieties!

PURPLE POTATOES

Originally from South America, potato plants have been cultivated for at least 5,000 years (some believe for as long as 8,000). Their cultivation became essential to indigenous communities across Peru, Bolivia, and much of the Andes.

During the last 500 years, the humble potato has been carried across the world and become the staple crop for hundreds of millions of people.

The large, pale tubers we know as potatoes are just a few of the thousands of types of potatoes still grown in South America. Across the Andes, potato tubers can be found in a startling spectrum of colors, from bright yellow to red, maroon, purple, black, and white.

They also vary in shape and size. Many varieties of potato have tiny, round tubers; others have knobbly ones shaped like pine cones; and yet others have long, pencil-shaped tubers (known as fingerling potatoes).

PURPLE CHIPS!

Many varieties of potatoes have deep blue-colored skins and flesh. These purple potatoes generally keep their unusual color when they are cooked, and so can be used to make bright purple chips!

DRAGON FRUIT

A PRETTY TOUGH CACTUS!

Dragon fruit are the large, striking, and rather refreshing fruit of the *Hylocereus* cactus. They are cultivated in the tropics around the world, but particularly in Southeast Asia, the Caribbean, and northern Australia. Their exact origins are uncertain, but the plants are native to Central America, occurring from southern Mexico through Belize, Guatemala, El Salvador, and Costa Rica. Two species of dragon fruit are commonly found, the white-fleshed *Hylocereus undatus* and the red-fleshed *H. costaricensis*.

These extraordinary fruit are produced from striking, succulent stems. They evolved in the deserts and subtropical regions of Central America where, at least in winter, nighttime temperatures can get very low. As a result, they can survive everything from mild frosts through heat waves of 105°F!

PRICKLY PEARS

The dragon fruit isn't the only species of cactus to have edible fruits. In fact, lots of other species do. The most widespread of all is the prickly pear, which produces pink or orange pear- or egg-shaped fruits at the end of its paddles. Prickly pear cacti have been grown for thousands of years as a crop, and in some parts of Mexico, it remains as important to local people as maize! Prickly pear fruit are also used to make delicious fruit drinks.

YELLOW MELONS

There are over 1,200 varieties of watermelon that are grown commercially. Some have black rinds; others have flesh that is bright yellow or tiny fruit that grow to just 6 inches in diameter! The yellow watermelons are a natural mutation and are known for their extremely sweet, honey-like taste. Other than their color and flavor, yellow watermelons are identical to the normal red varieties.

SUPER-SHAPED WATERMELONS

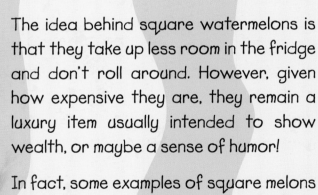

Horticulturists in Japan have perfected the art of growing watermelons in molds to shape the fruit into particular shapes. The most well known of these are "square watermelons". They can fetch very high prices in Japan, some selling for the equivalent of US$10,000!

The idea behind square watermelons is that they take up less room in the fridge and don't roll around. However, given how expensive they are, they remain a luxury item usually intended to show wealth, or maybe a sense of humor!

In fact, some examples of square melons aren't even edible as they are not always fully developed when harvested. Ultimately, these fruit are a novelty decorative item that can truly surprise onlookers. Provided you can find a good quality mold, you can grow your own in your garden!

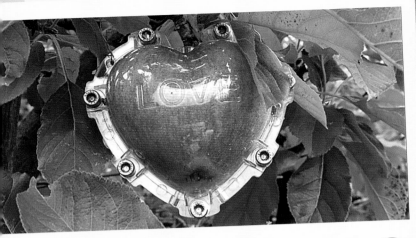

AMAZING APPLES

It is possible to grow almost any soft fruit into unusual shapes using molds. Apples work really well, although you will need a much smaller mold than that used for watermelons! Apple trees are very easy to grow and produce fruit even when grown as patio plants in tubs. Ask your parents or teachers if you can grow an apple tree at home or school to create your own super-shaped fruit.

SKULL FRUIT!

Watermelons have been grown into various shapes, including cubes, perfect spheres, hearts, and even skulls! Some have been grown to resemble statues of the Buddha! These shapes are created by placing developing fruit in molds — it has nothing to do with genetics, only technique!

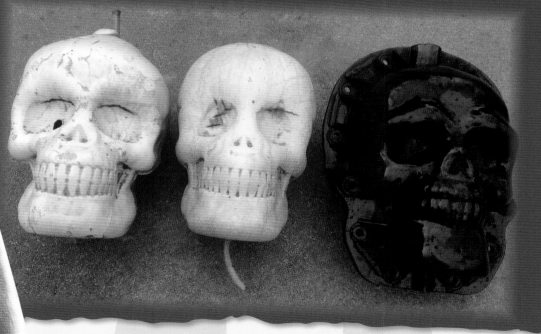

Cucamelons

Also known as mouse melons or Mexican sour gherkins, cucamelons (*Melothria scabra*) are grape-sized members of the cucumber and melon family that taste of cucumber with a hint of lime, a flavor that becomes stronger as fruit are left to develop. They are one of the cutest-looking foods there is, making them very popular!

Cucamelons are native to Central America, and in Mexico are known as *sandiitas de ratón*, which means "little mouse watermelons". The fruits are only about 1.5 inches long and are striped like watermelons, accounting for this common name. Although they are not commonly grown, they are increasingly popular because they have a pleasant flavor, are easy to grow (and quite drought tolerant), and are mostly ignored by common plant pests.

SNAKE FRUIT

The snake fruit is so called because it is lined with scales that look exactly like the skin of a snake!

It is actually the fruit of a type of palm from South-east Asia. In Indonesia, it is known as "salak", and hundreds of types of snake fruit are cultivated and sold!

RED BANANAS

There are about 70 species of bananas, most of which come from the rainforests of Asia.

The seedless yellow bananas that we all are familiar with are actually complex hybrids that were bred to yield optimal fruit.

But there are also many wild and cultivated types of bananas that produce delicious bright red fruit such as *Musa acuminata* (shown here).

LIFE-GIVING LEAVES

Leaves are truly amazing.

We see leaves so frequently that we often take them for granted, the countless blades of grass in a lawn or the foliage of a tree.

But stop and think about leaves ... as power generators that create life-giving energy from carbon dioxide, water, and sunlight!

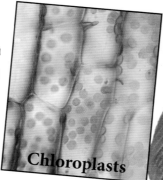

Chloroplasts

Imagine if you never had to eat but could get all of the energy you needed from sun bathing!

It is all thanks to the process of photosynthesis that takes place in the chloroplasts of cells in plant leaves (see page 15). Most leaves have an incredibly complex structure!

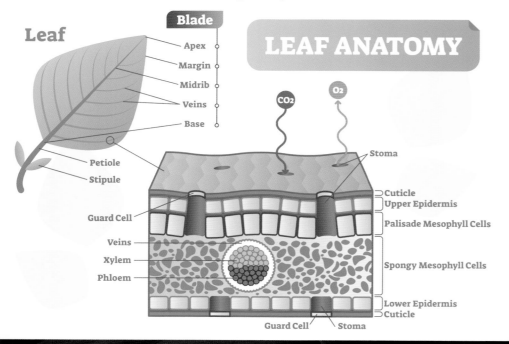

Leaf

Blade
- Apex
- Margin
- Midrib
- Veins
- Base
- Petiole
- Stipule

LEAF ANATOMY

CO₂ O₂

- Stoma
- Guard Cell
- Veins
- Xylem
- Phloem
- Cuticle
- Upper Epidermis
- Palisade Mesophyll Cells
- Spongy Mesophyll Cells
- Lower Epidermis
- Cuticle
- Guard Cell
- Stoma

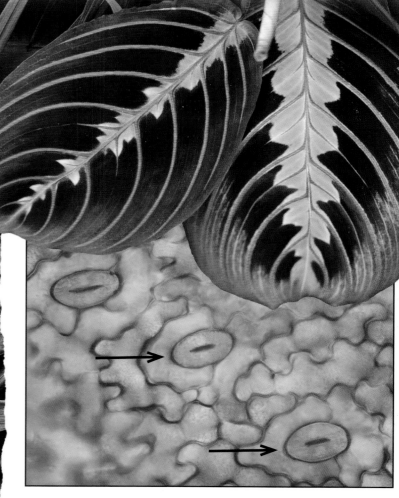

STOMATA

Did you know plants breathe via tiny pores on their leaves called stomata? They allow carbon dioxide to diffuse into the leaves during the day (for photosynthesis) and oxygen during the night (for respiration).

TYPES OF LEAVES

With very few exceptions, plants must photosynthesize to survive; otherwise they "starve" for lack of energy.

Most leaves, therefore, evolved to catch light as efficiently as possible, usually as broad structures positioned perpendicular to the direction of light.

Lots of factors influence leaf designs. Plants that grow in wet environments often have filamentous foliage or "drip tips" to drain away water that would otherwise clog stomata.

Many plants produce pigments in their leaves, resulting in foliage that can be every color and pattern imaginable.

A few plants are carnivorous and produce highly specialized leaves that attract, catch, kill, and digest insects and other small animals!

LEAF VEINS

Look at a leaf under a magnifying glass and you may notice countless intricate little lines. These are called veins.

The veins strengthen the structure of a leaf and contain "transport tissues" which carry water, nutrients, and energy. This transport mechanism is known as the plant's vascular system.

Generally, veins have two types of vascular tissues:

Xylem tissues move water and nutrients from the plant's roots upward to the stem, leaves, and flowers.

Phloem tissues move food energy (made during photosynthesis) to the parts of the plant where it is needed.

Many leaves also have a prominent central vein which is called the midrib. This is important as it gives leaves structural strength. Without a midrib, most leaves would droop.

The presence or absence of a vascular system distinguishes many large groups of plants (see page 12). All seed-bearing plants are vascular, but several families of spore-producing plants lack veins entirely!

Have you ever found a leaf skeleton in autumn? A few weeks after the leaves have fallen from the trees, look on the ground, especially in wet places, and you might find a leaf where all of the tissues except the tough veins have rotted away!

Place your leaf skeleton onto a piece of black paper and you will see the incredible intricacy of the fine leaf veins! Just think; this level of detail is all around you, in every single leaf of every tree that you see!

AUTUMN COLORS

Have you seen the leaves of trees change color in autumn?

The foliage of many tree species from the northern hemisphere (such as maples and acers) transforms from green to burning shades of red, orange, and yellow.

This is a response to the days growing shorter and colder as winter approaches. The trees cut their losses and suspend photosynthesis during the dark winter months. The leaves shut down and the valuable chlorophyll is withdrawn, revealing the pigments and waste products in the leaf tissues, which causes entire landscapes to flush with autumnal colors.

IRIDESCENT -LEAVED PLANTS

Most leaves are green because they contain chlorophyll, the chemical used in photosynthesis. But a few species of plants from tropical areas across South America, Africa, and Asia produce leaves that sparkle electric blue like peacock feathers. This iridescent blue shine is not a pigment, but an optical effect produced by reflected light.

In most iridescent-leaved plants, the upper surface of the foliage shines a brilliant blue color that is visible only from certain angles. Although lots of theories have been put forward, botanists do not know for certain why plants have iridescent leaves. It is not merely a way to attract pollinators, since iridescent-leaved plants include ferns which do not flower.

It may be that the iridescent shine serves to protect the leaves by reflecting the higher levels of ultraviolet (blue) light which are found at higher elevations, where many of the iridescent-leaved plants grow.

Concentrated ultraviolet light is known to have a damaging effect on the chloroplasts of most plant species, and some of the iridescent-leaved plants grow on mountain summits exposed to very strong sunlight. Perhaps by reflecting the blue component of sunlight, the iridescent plants have evolved a form of natural sunscreen. But other iridescent-leaved plants grow in dense shade and still have a blue shine.

These beautiful plants are even more mysterious because, when brought into cultivation, the brilliance of the shine is often lost or greatly reduced, even if cultivated plants are grown in conditions that accurately reflect the natural environment of the wild.

STAINED GLASS WINDOW PLANT

The tropical rainforests of South America are home to the stained glass window plant (*Columnea consanguinea*).

It is so-called because it has bright red, heart-shaped, translucent markings on the underside of its leaves. Light shines through these patches just like stained glass windows in a church!

The plant's "windows" act just like colorful petals on a flower. They advertise the presence of small, tubular flowers that are borne near the base of the stained glass window plant's leaves.

A beautiful little hummingbird called the green-crowned brilliant is attracted by the red "windows" and acts as the plant's main pollinator.

SENSITIVE PLANTS

The sensitive plant (*Mimosa pudica*) is a little scrambling plant from Central and South America. It forms a woody stem up to 5 feet long and has little prickles along its stem and branches.

Its foliage is carried on short branches and, amazingly, when touched, the leaflets rapidly fold together (normally within less than a second).

If touched a second time, the branches quickly droop downward (also within a second or so)!

WHY IT MOVES

It is believed that the foliage of the plant responds in this way to deter leaf-eating insects, for as soon as they climb on the leaves, their meal folds up and disappears!

Contact with any object can cause the leaves to close. Usually, all of the leaves of a sensitive plant close during a rainstorm.

After stimulation, the foliage reopens a few minutes or hours later. Generally, the more sunlight and the healthier the plant, the faster the reaction time of the leaves! All the leaves close when it gets dark each evening and reopen in the morning light.

LITTLE TREE PLANT

The little tree plant (*Biophytum sensitivum*) is so-called because it resembles a palm tree but grows just 8 inches tall. It comes from Nepal, India, and other parts of Asia.

It also has sensitive leaves, and when stimulated, the leaflets fold downward (although more slowly than the sensitive plant – taking a few seconds to fold completely)!

Many species of carnivorous plants have leaves that move really quickly to trap prey! The leaves of the Venus's flytrap snap shut to imprison insects. The leaves of sticky sundew and butterworts wrap around victims, and bladderworts suck in prey!

TRAMPOLINE SEED DISPERSAL

The seed pods of the little tree plant open quickly and can fling out seeds as they do so.

Once open, the pods form a star-shaped trampoline that faces toward the sky. Falling raindrops splash on the surface of the trampoline and bounce the little seeds from the pods! This helps the little tree plant spread to new habitats nearby!

Other plants produce cup-shaped seed pods (called "splash cups") that catch raindrops. In a similar way to the trampoline, the falling drops also splash the seeds to new nearby habitats.

EXPLODING SEED PODS!

Many plants produce seed pods that "explode" to scatter their seeds away from the mother plant!

One of the best examples is the Himalayan balsam (*Impatiens glandulifera*). It produces attractive white, pink, or light purple flowers which, when pollinated, form hanging pear-shaped pods.

The ripe pods are extremely sensitive. At the slightest touch, the sides recoil in a fraction of a second, flinging the seeds up to 21 feet away!

This seed dispersal mechanism is so effective that the Himalayan balsam has spread from the Himalayas and has now become an invasive weed across Europe and North America!

seed pods ready to explode!

an exploded seed pod

SEED DISPERSAL

The more widely plants can disperse their seeds, the greater the chances they have to keep control of the habitat in which they grow and the greater their chance of colonizing new areas of habitat.

Flying and gliding seeds, splash cups, exploding seed pods, and squirting fruit are all methods of distributing seed as widely as possible!

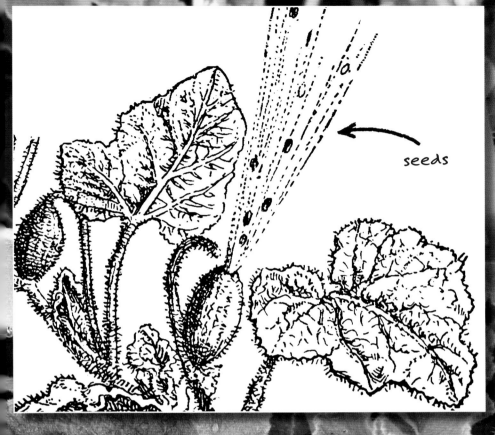

seeds

SQUIRTING CUCUMBER

The squirting cucumber (*Ecballium elaterium*) is native to Europe and parts of temperate Africa and Asia.

It produces a scrambling stem up to 5 feet long, with triangular leaves and small, bell-shaped flowers.

When the flowers are pollinated, 1.5 inch long seed pods develop. The mature pods are filled with a jelly-like liquid under high pressure. The slightest movement causes the pods to detach from the stem.

As they detach, the pressurized liquid jets out from a hole in each pod. This causes the pods to blast away like little rockets. In the process, the seeds are squirted up to 18 feet away!

GREENHOUSE PLANTS

Plants often have very clever ways to survive in extreme conditions.

Growing in the highlands of Tibet, at over 13,000 feet, two plants (*Saussurea medusa* and *Rheum alexandrae*) use their leaves to create their own greenhouses!

In *Saussurea medusa* (below), the whole plant grows as a compact ball of foliage. Dense hairs develop between the leaves and completely insulate the plant, creating an appearance a bit like a sea urchin. The temperature inside is several degrees warmer, just like the inside of a greenhouse!

In *Rheum alexandrae* (below), large, expanded, cream-colored leaves cover the flowers, protecting them from exposure to the wind and cold. This allows the plant to grow as a 3 foot tall tower!

Through these remarkable adaptations, both species can live in landscapes of almost bare rock, where few other plant species can survive.

BEAUTIFUL BROMELIADS

The bromeliad family includes many interesting plants that often grow on the branches of trees (epiphytes).

There are about 3,500 species of bromeliads, which occur across tropical and subtropical areas of the Americas, although there is just one species that also occurs in tropical West Africa.

You may have eaten a bromeliad recently! The pineapple (*Ananas comosus*) is a bromeliad and the only one that is edible!

AMAZING COLORS

Most bromeliads have tiny flowers nestled among very colorful and striking scapes! In many species the leaves also turn bright colors.

A PLANT WITH A POOL!

Bromeliads range greatly in size. The smallest are only a few inches tall, while the biggest can be enormous (see page 121). Most species are 8–18 inches across.

Growing on the branches of trees, most bromeliads do not have roots, like those of most plants that grow into soil to absorb nutrients and water. As such, in many species (known as "tank bromeliads"), the center of the rosette forms a little pool.

The pool is topped up by rainwater and collects dead leaves. This provides the plant with water and nutrients.

Many animals, particularly frogs, live in the bromeliads' pools or use them to rear their young. Larger bromeliads may have an entire ecosystem in their pools!

AIRPLANTS

The bromeliad family includes a group of about 650 species of "airplants" (*Tillandsia*) from tropical and subtropical parts of the Americas.

Most airplants grow as epiphytes (plants that grow on other plants), and they may festoon the branches of their host trees.

Airplants get virtually all of the nutrients and water they need from their leaves.

Their foliage is covered with little white, hair-like structures called trichomes. These increase their surface area to boost nutrient and water absorption from the air, rain, dew, and any dust or dead leaves that fall on the plants.

trichomes

The roots are only used to anchor the airplants onto the branch or tree trunk where they grow.

Airplants are so called because they usually do not need soil. They come in many strange shapes and forms, often as balls of short, spiky leaves. Most have long, narrow leaves.

Most species change color when they flower and turn brilliant shades of bright red or pink to attract moths, hummingbirds, and even bats, which act as pollinators.

Airplants are easy and fun to grow at home. As they do not need soil, they can be grown almost anywhere, although growing them on bathroom windowsills, in conservatories, and, shady greenhouses works particularly well. Most species like dappled sunlight, high humidity, and warm conditions (50°–90°F).

Airplants produce some of the most unusual foliage and striking flower scapes of all bromeliads!

One of the strangest species is called *Tillandsia bulbosa*. It produces a bulbous stem with long, snake-like arms! When it flowers, the uppermost leaves and the flower scape can turn bright red as the small, purple flowers emerge. The rest of the plant remains dark green. The leaf bases of *Tillandsia bulbosa* are hollow and often are home to nests of ants, which may protect the plant from herbivorous insects in return for their home!

Most airplants (and bromeliads in general) flower only once and then die. But often, new plants sprout from the base of the mother plant as it withers away. The sprouting plants are known as "pups" and often two, three, or four form at a time. As each pup then matures and flowers (then dies and produces more pups), many airplants form dense clumps.

Just like the tank bromeliads (see previous pages), many airplants also capture water and leaf litter in the center of their leaf rosettes.

SPANISH MOSS

An unusual species of airplant called Spanish moss (*Tillandsia usneoides*) grows across the southern United States and much of the Caribbean.

It grows as trailing tufts that hang from branches. Spanish moss may completely cloak host trees and has earned the name "grandpa's beard" because of its appearance! Unlike most airplants, it has yellow flowers.

WATER PROTECTION

Cacti are highly adapted to surviving in deserts, and unlike most plant species, grow as a stem without typical photosynthesizing leaves.

There are over 1,750 species of cacti, and all come from the Americas. Some are enormous, such as the massive saguaro cactus (*Carnegiea gigantea*) which stands 36 feet tall, can live for 150 years, and can weigh 4,800 pounds! Others may be just a few inches tall.

In most cacti, the stem itself is green and makes energy from sunlight.

The lack of leaves reduces the amount of water that the cactus needs in order to survive. Cacti also have far fewer pores (stomata) than most plants, and the outer surface of their stems is waxy. These further help to reduce water loss.

Some cacti species are lined with woolly white hairs which reflect intense desert sunlight and heat. All of these adaptations help enable cacti to survive in arid environments.

Most cacti have spongy tissues that store water very efficiently. In many cacti, the stems are pleated, allowing the cactus to expand rapidly as it absorbs water when rain does fall. This enables large cacti to store literally tons of water for months at a time!

Water is very precious in arid habitats, and many animals would eat cactus plants if they could. Most cacti defend themselves by producing spines. The spines are actually highly modified leaves. In some species, they are tiny and break off, causing irritation in victims. In others, the spines are rigid and up to 8 inches long!

Generally, there are relatively few pollinators in the arid habitats where cacti grow, so many of them produce large and brightly colored flowers to attract the few pollinators that there are.

For decades, horticulturists have grafted mutant strains of cacti (particularly *Gymnocalycium mihanovichii*) that lack chlorophyll (and so appear bright red, orange, or yellow) onto another cactus plant (below, right).

SPINES AND STINGS

Through photosynthesis, plants create energy, which fuels virtually all life on Earth. Almost all animals depend upon plants to survive (either by eating them or eating animals that eat plants). But plants have evolved many ways to defend themselves from the attacks of animals.

Many plants have poisonous saps, while others have ferocious spines, sometimes backwards-pointing barbs that make the spines especially painful (for example, brambles)! A few plants cover their leaves with sharp needles that have chemicals that deliver a painful sting (such as stinging nettles). Plants with these adaptations are often spared by herbivores!

bramble spikes

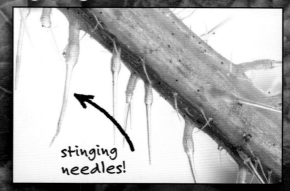

sharp spines

stinging nettle spines

stinging needles!

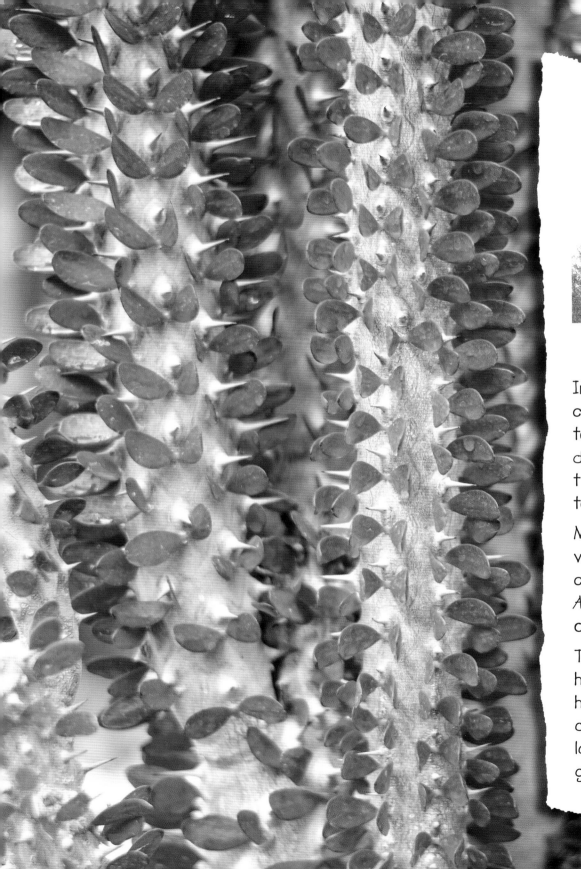

SPINY FOREST

In Madagascar, a unique ecosystem has evolved called "spiny forest". Similar (but unrelated) to cacti, the plants of the spiny forest have developed sharp spines to protect the water they store in their tissues, but they take spines to the extreme!

More so than any other biome on Earth, the vegetation of the spiny forest is absolutely covered in spines! The dominant plants are often *Alluaudia* spp. (known as "octopus trees" because of their arm-like branches that reach to the sky).

The octopus trees have rows of tiny leaves hidden among sharp spines, protecting them from herbivores. Amazingly, lemurs live in the spiny forest and jump between the octopus trees, somehow landing on the extremely spiny branches without getting prickled!

⚠ WARNING

While stinging nettles may cause a painful sting, in Australia, there is a group of plants whose stings can be truly dangerous.

Known as "stinging trees", one species, *Dendrocnide moroides*, has perhaps the most powerful sting of all. Its sting is so painful that it has been known to kill dogs and horses, and drive humans mad with agony.

Stinging trees are covered with tiny needles that are so fine they can't be removed with tweezers. Just brushing against the large, heart-shaped leaves causes the sting, which botanist Marina Hurley described as "being burned by hot acid and electrocuted at the same time".

Cyril Bromley, another victim of the stinging tree, had to be strapped to a hospital bed for three weeks because of the pain caused by falling into a patch of leaves. The stinging trees' defenses are enough to deter most herbivores, although some insects are immune to the stings.

stinging nettle

white dead nettle

MIMICRY

Some plants use mimicry to pretend to have stings without expending the energy to produce them! The stinging nettle has distinctive jagged-edged leaves, but an unrelated plant called the white dead nettle (*Urtica dioica*) has evolved exactly the same leaf shape! Most herbivores avoid it (even though its leaves are completely harmless). However, its flowers give it away!

ANT DEFENDERS

Acacias are a diverse group of tropical trees that are widespread across Africa and Australia.

Many species have ferocious spines to deter herbivores, but some have special relationships with ants as well! The bullhorn tree has swollen hollow spines shaped like the horns of a bull. Ants with powerful bites live in the horns and, when a herbivore tries to eat the tree's leaves, the ants emerge and attack!

Some acacias have specialized glands that release honeydew (a sweet liquid food) for their ant defenders. Others even produce beads of food on the ends of their leaflets for the ants!

hollow spines (home to ants)

honeydew wells

AMAZING PLANTS

Plants are amazing! They are the ultimate survivors, growing in some of the hottest and driest corners of the globe as well as some of the world's wettest and coldest regions.

Plants can be found as high as 20,000 feet, at altitudes where few animals can survive. They include the most massive organisms on the planet, as well as the longest-lived ones, which can grow for thousands of years.

The diversity of shapes, forms, and survival strategies of plants is almost endless. Their flowers and leaves come in every color and design imaginable. In this chapter, we will explore some of the most spectacular plants of all!

CLASSIFICATION

There are many groups of plants alive today on Earth (see pages 12 and 13). By far the most diverse and numerous are the flowering plants (which include around 318,000 species). Botanists classify plants by the structure of their foliage and reproductive parts.

TYPES OF FLOWERING PLANTS

Flowering plants can be classified into several distinctive groups based on the flower structure. A few of the main groups include:

<u>Asteraceae</u> (daisy family), which includes about 32,000 known species (and over 1,900 genera). They typically produce circular flowers consisting of lots of individual flower "florets".

<u>Orchids</u>, differentiated from virtually all other flowering plants by the fusion of the male portion of the flower (stamen) and female portion (pistil) into one structure called the column (often visible protruding from the center). Over 28,000 species, comprising at least 760 genera, are known worldwide.

<u>Aroids (also known as arums)</u> have distinctive flowers borne on a type of inflorescence called a spadix (a pointy structure at the center). The spadix is usually enclosed in a spathe (leaf-like bract). There are over 2,750 species.

<u>Bromeliads</u> have septal nectaries, inferior ovaries, and usually trichomes on their leaves. The bromeliad family comprises over 4,000 species.

AWESOME ORCHIDS!

Orchids are the second largest group of flowering plants and perhaps the most famous!

Many species produce large leaves and striking, colorful flowers. One incredible species of slipper orchid (*Paphiopedilum sanderianum*, shown here, see right) has curly petals that can measure over 3 feet long!

Other species (known as "micro orchids") produce flowers that are as small as 0.3 inches across and a leaf rosette 1 inch across.

Orchids produce the tiniest seeds of all flowering plants (often 0.1 inches). A single seed pod may contain 3 million or more seeds!

VANILLA

Most orchids form partnerships with fungi, which entwine around the orchid's roots and facilitate the absorption of nutrients and water. This symbiosis is called a mycorrhizal association, and is often essential for the orchid's growth and survival.

Orchids produce such vast numbers of tiny dust-like seeds to increase the chances of the seeds landing and coming into contact with a suitable fungal partner as they germinate.

Horticulturists have cultivated and bred orchids for centuries, and over 100,000 hybrids have been produced to date!

You have eaten an orchid recently! There is just a single orchid species that is grown commercially ... vanilla orchid (*Vanilla planifolia*). It produces seed pods which are dried to produce "vanilla beans". The pods contain countless tiny seeds. When cured, the pods have an incredible aromatic flavor. Today, vanilla is used in countless products, including soda, chocolate, coffee, and baked goods!

Dragons Blood Tree

The remote island of Socotra in the Arabian Sea is home to the striking dragons blood tree (*Dracaena cinnabari*). It is named after the blood-like color of the red sap that the trees produce.

The dragons blood tree has a very unusual appearance. It produces densely packed, highly divided branches that take the form of an upside-down umbrella. The "dragons blood" resin was highly prized across the ancient world, used as a dye, medicine, and for magical rituals, sometimes traded for its weight in gold!

Ghost Pipes

Ghost pipe plants (also known as Indian pipes, *Monotropa uniflora*) are native to Asia and North America. Unlike most plants, they do not produce chlorophyll, so are ghostly white!

Ghost pipes are parasitic and obtain all the water and nutrients they need from fungal partners, which in turn often siphon their food from trees. Since ghost pipes are not dependent on sunlight to grow, they can often be found growing on the dark floor of dense forests!

LIVING FOSSILS

A living fossil is a species that has remained unchanged over millions of years, so that it (or close relatives) is alive today but is also known from the fossil record!

Many species of plants can truly be called living fossils.

One of the best known examples is the unique tree *Ginkgo biloba* (see page 13 and leaves shown above right). Very similar fossils extend back to the Middle Jurassic, over 170 million years ago!

Similarly, the wollemia pine (*Wollemia nobilis*) is almost indistinguishable from fossils dated to the Cretaceous period (some 90 million years ago), and trees of the genus *Araucaria* resemble fossils that are over 100 million years old.

Some evidence suggests that the long necks of sauropod dinosaurs may have evolved specifically to browse the foliage of tall *Araucaria* trees!

gingko

wollemia pine

horsetails

Land plants first appeared around 450 million years ago during the Ordovician period. Some of the very earliest were bryophytes (including liverworts, hornworts, and mosses). Many species of these groups survive today and resemble 200 million year old fossils.

One of the oldest lineages of living vascular plants are lycopods, which appeared during the Silurian period (425 million years ago).

Several living species of lycopods closely resemble fossils that are over 250 million years old (dating back to times before the dinosaurs appeared). Additionally, many species of horsetails, ferns, and cycads are similarly unchanged since the late Jurassic (165 million years ago) or earlier.

It is incredible to consider the expanses of time during which these plants have existed. The continents moved and reshaped, the dinosaurs came and went, and still these plants remain, more or less unchanged through the ages.

cycads

What on Earth? The Plants You Have Never Heard Of

leaves close up at night

HIGH ALTITUDE PLANTS

Cushion plants have recently been found growing at over 20,000 feet on mountains in India! Such plants living in high altitude environments require extreme adaptations in order to survive.

In South America, the Andes are home to distinctive, tower-like *Espeletia* (page 94). The foliage of these plants is covered with insulating woolly hairs that protect the leaves from high ultra violet light, extremely cold conditions, and savage wind exposure. Dead leaves remain attached to the stem to protect and insulate the vascular tissues, like cladding on a pipe!

In Africa, on Mount Kilimanjaro, the giant groundsel (*Dendrosenecio kilimanjari*) has a special trick. Its leaf rosettes close up during the night to protect the delicate central growth points!

PARASITES!

Some plants steal food from other plants! These are known as parasites.

Rafflesia are parasitic plants from Asia that live inside a host vine. There are approximately 28 species, none of which produce leaves or any other visible parts except flowers and fruit.

They live as a network of fiber-like tissues within their host vine, and steal all the energy they need to produce gigantic flowers (see page 118).

The related genera *Sapria* and *Balanophora* have similar parasitic lifestyles.

STRANGLER VINE

Dodder is a group of parasitic plants of the genus *Cuscuta*, belonging to the morning glory family.

It lacks visible leaves and grows as a thin thread. Once it detects the chemical signature of another plant, it grows in tight coils around its victim and produces root-like structures called haustoria. These penetrate its host's tissues and steal all of the nutrients and water the dodder needs!

Over time, dodder plants grow all over their victims, earning their common name devil's hair!

STRANGLER FIG

Strangler figs start life as tiny seeds deposited by animals in the crook of a tree or on its branches. On germination, the fig sends out roots that snake down the trunk of the host tree or dangle as aerial roots.

Once the roots reach the ground, the fig grows quickly. It produces a network of roots that encircle the host tree and fuse together. As the roots thicken, they squeeze the host's trunk and cut off its flow of nutrients. Eventually the host is killed and rots, and the strangler fig absorbs the resulting nutrients, leaving only a hollow lattice of the fig's roots!

SPECTACULAR SUCCULENTS

Succulents are plants that are adapted to growing in dry areas of the world by producing thick fleshy leaves and stems that store water.

Cacti are the best known succulents, but there are hundreds of unrelated groups of plants that botanists include together.

Many species of succulents produce compact, low-growing, colorful rosettes of thick, fleshy leaves, often with white or pearly bands and blotches. Some do not produce any leaves at all but have evolved swollen stems to photosynthesize (for example, most cacti species).

Succulents are often really colorful and interesting to grow at home. *Aloes*, *Euphorbia*, and *Kalanchoe* are among the more popular upright-growing succulents, and many of these produce intricate foliage with unusual forms, shapes, and colors.

FLOWERS IN ARID LANDS

Many species of aloes have evolved bright red, tubular flowers that are highly adapted to pollination by sunbirds.

The sunbirds visit the flowers to collect nectar. However, the nectaries are positioned deep inside the structure of the flowers.

In order to reach the sugary nectar, the sunbird has to reach deep into the bloom with its beak.

Since the aloe's reproductive parts are positioned at the opening of each flower, as the sunbird reaches inside, it receives a dab of pollen on its head. If it visits another aloe flower, it delivers the pollen, bringing about fertilization!

What on Earth? The Plants You Have Never Heard Of!

QUIVER TREES

Quiver trees (*Aloe dichotoma*) are a species of aloe native to South Africa and Namibia. They grow in extremely dry habitats where rain may fall just a few times each year.

Like many succulent plants, they have reflective white bark (to reduce the absorption of heat) and small, leathery leaves with few pores (to reduce the loss of water through respiration).

But they also have two special survival tricks.

In severe drought, the quiver tree can "self-amputate" some of its rosettes of foliage. Corky tissue seals the veins in a few of its branches, causing some of the leaf rosettes to eventually break off and fall to the ground. With luck, the tree may survive the dry times with a reduced number of leaves, and will put out new branch shoots when the rains return.

The inside of the quiver tree's trunk and branches consists of a spongy tissue which rapidly absorbs water, so when the rains do arrive, the tree can absorb and store as much water as possible. This store of water allows it to survive periods of months with no rain at all.

San Bushmen used to hollow out the spongy tissue of the branches to make quivers for their arrows, which is how the tree gets its name!

EUPHORBIAS

Cacti occur exclusively in the Americas, with one exception (*Hipsalis baccifera*), which occurs in parts of Africa and Asia.

Many other groups of succulents evolved in different parts of the world that superficially look very similar to cacti and have essentially the same adaptations to survive drought.

Euphorbias are widespread across southern Africa and Madagascar. Like cacti, many *Euphorbias* lack leaves and have pillar-shaped stems armed with large, defensive spines.

But *Euphorbias* also have a trick that most cacti lack! Many species have milky sap that is often extremely poisonous.

The sap can be so toxic that in the 19th century, settlers in Africa died after cooking meat on a fire burning *Euphorbia* wood! The smoke can be lethal if inhaled and contaminated their food!

WINDOW PLANTS

Window plants (*Fenestraria* spp.) grow in the arid lands of Namibia and South Africa, where the summers are very hot and dry.

Each window plant produces thick leaves that have completely clear windows on top. The window plant grows underground except for the leaf tops, which poke just through the ground's surface.

Sunlight shines into the thick leaves, passing through the clear windows and onto chlorophyll-rich tissues at the leaf bases below ground. This enables the window plant to photosynthesize even though it is buried. This growth habit enables the window plant to remain hidden from herbivores and protected from extreme heat.

A few species of *Haworthia* have similar transparent sections at the tips of their leaves and can function like the window plant even when covered in sand!

LIVING STONES

The pebble plant (*Lithops*) comes from South Africa and Namibia, and grows underground except for two thick leaves that emerge above the level of the soil and are colored to look just like pebbles! The plant is a master of disguise, and is both camouflaged from animals that might like to eat it and protected under the soil from the extreme heat of the desert!

There are many species of pebble plants that vary in shape, size, color, and texture to match the stones that occur in their natural habitats.

Spotting these plants in the wild can be very tricky unless they are flowering! Most have yellow or white blooms.

ICE PLANTS

High levels of salt can be lethal to most plants. This makes many coastal habitats, lashed by salty ocean spray, unsuitable for lots of plant species.

But the ice plant (*Mesembryanthemum crystallinum*) has a clever way of growing in saline habitats.

It is covered with enlarged "bladder cells", which store the salt that is removed from the plant's tissues. The bladder cells also serve as a water reserve for the plant to use during times of drought.

The bladder cells make the ice plant look as though it is covered in frost, even though it grows in hot, dry parts of Africa, Europe, and the Middle East!

ANT PLANTS

Ant plants (*Myrmecodia* spp.) have evolved a special partnership with ants which enables them to grow in habitats where most other plants would perish for lack of nutrients.

They are mainly found across Southeast Asia and cling to the branches of trees. They have greatly swollen stems that may be as much as 24 inches across! The stem is a honeycomb of hollow, interconnected chambers which offer the perfect home for ants!

The ants use one of the chambers inside the ant plant for their queen, others for rearing worker ants, and a few chambers are designated as storage dumps, where the ants deposit their droppings and even their dead!

The ant plant absorbs nutrients from the refuse in the storage chambers. This enables the ant plant to grow as an epiphyte (with none of its roots touching the ground).

In return for their home, the ants defend the ant plant from herbivores! Below is a dissected ant plant showing the chambers.

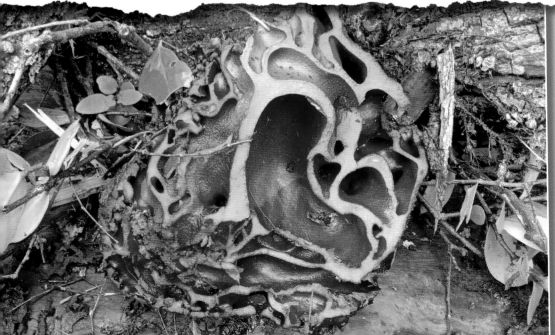

GIANT WATERLILIES

The giant Amazon waterlily (*Victoria amazonica*) is the world's largest species of waterlily. It produces leaves up to 9 feet in diameter that float on the water surface, attached to the plant by a stalk that may be up to 25 feet long.

The undersurface of the leaves has struts which form chambers that naturally fill up with air and give each pad buoyancy. Each leaf can support over 144 pounds in weight, allowing children to sit on the floating leaves without sinking!

SEAGRASS

Seagrasses are the only flowering plants that grow in the ocean. There are about 60 species worldwide, which mostly occur in shallow waters at tropical and temperate latitudes.

They produce narrow leaves which grow by rhizome extension and spread across large "meadows" resembling grassland on land.

Amazingly, most species of seagrasses undergo pollination under water! Male seagrass flowers release pollen into the water. Seagrasses produce the longest pollen grains of all plants (up to 0.2 inches). The pollen is moved by underwater currents until it lands on the pistil of a female flower and fertilization takes place. The fertilized seagrass then produces seed.

Just like meadows on land, many animals graze seagrass beds, including sea turtles, dugongs, and manatees. These aquatic plants are extremely important for marine ecosystems.

RECORD HOLDERS

THE PLANT WITH THE BIGGEST LEAF

There are many ways to categorize leaves, but the raffia palm (*Raphia farinifera*) of the Mascarene Islands has the largest leaves of any plant. They can reach 80 feet long by 9 feet wide, but are made up of around 180 separate leaflets.

The biggest undivided leaf of all is produced by the elephant ear plant (*Alocasia robusta*) from Borneo (below). One was measured to be over 9 feet long and 6 feet wide, although there are reports of this species producing leaves over 14 feet long and 8 feet wide!

Several giant-leaved *Anthurium* species may produce leaves nearly as large too, such as *Anthurium metalicum* and *A. salgarense*.

Such enormous leaves can only arise in tropical areas where the temperature is constantly warm. Freezing conditions would destroy the vascular tissues of such enormous leaves, which explains why there aren't giant-leaved plants in temperate regions.

THE WORLD'S TALLEST TREE

The tallest trees in the world are coast redwoods (*Sequoia sempervirens*), which tower above the ground in California and southwestern Oregon.

These gigantic trees typically grow to over 300 feet. A particularly tall specimen, named Hyperion, was discovered in 2006 and measured 380 feet in 2009, making it the tallest tree alive on the planet!

The world's most massive tree (largest by volume) is the giant sequoia (*Sequoiadendron giganteum*) from California. The largest known tree alive today is named General Sherman. It has been estimated to be over 52,500 feet^3 in volume, about 2,000 years old, and 272 feet tall. One was cut down in 1905 which was reported to have had a volume of 88,000 ft^3! Redwoods are so large that tunnels for cars have been carved through them!

THE WORLD'S BIGGEST KELP

Kelps are not plants, but instead belong to a separate grouping of organisms called heterokonts. Nevertheless, they do photosynthesize energy from the sun much like true plants, and form immense underwater forests.

Giant kelp (*Macrocystis pyrifera*) produces stalks that can grow 150 feet in length, buoyed up by floats. The stalks of kelp are longer than the leaves of any true plants.

Giant kelp is among the fastest-growing organisms on Earth. Each stalk can grow at a rate of 24 inches each day over the growing season.

Giant kelp forms rich habitats for a variety of marine life. Many species of fish use the stalks as nursery areas, while starfish and sea urchins graze around the kelp's holdfasts at its base.

FASTEST
GROWING LAND PLANTS

The world record for the fastest growing land plant belongs to a strain of bamboo called "beema bamboo" (*Bambusa balcooa*). It has been reported that shoots of beema bamboo can grow up to 3 feet per day (0.02 mph)!

Bamboos belong to the grass family. Their stems are chambered and mostly hollow, which partly explains why their tissues can expand rapidly when growing.

Among the approximately 1,000 species of bamboo, several grow to a height of 120 feet or more.

It is fortunate that many species of bamboo grow quickly because they are the main food of pandas, who eat lots of bamboo every day!

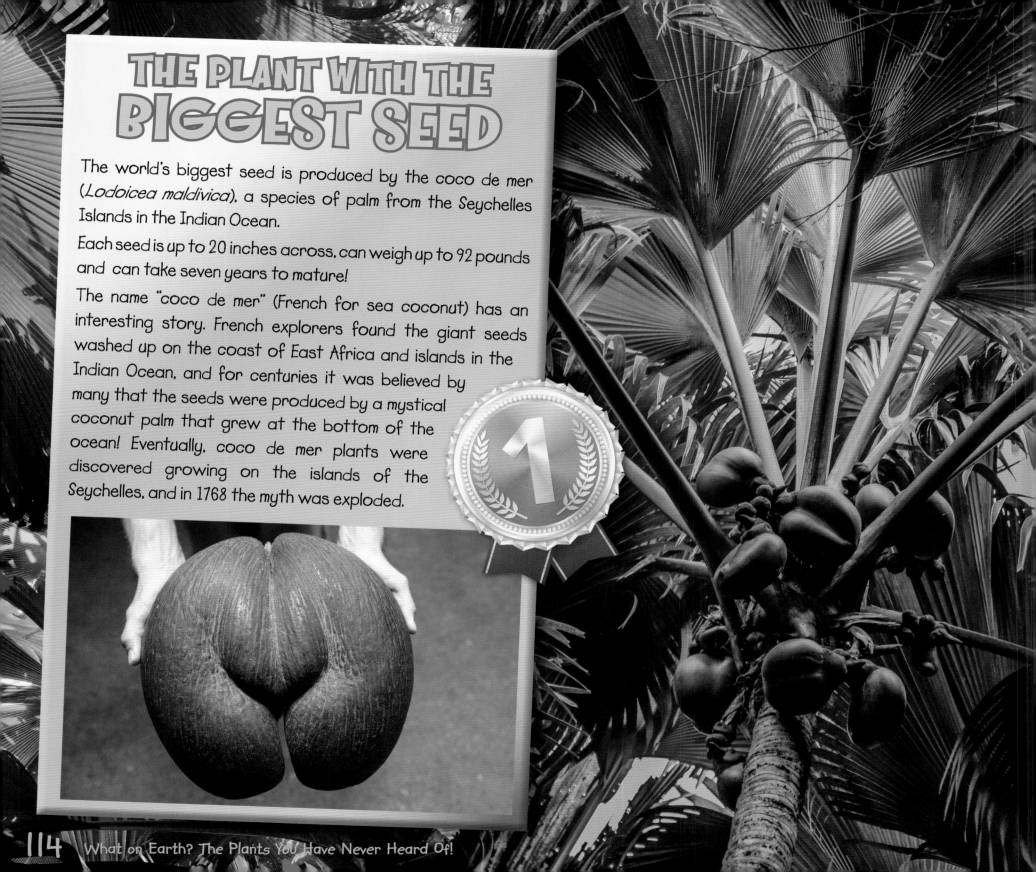

THE PLANT WITH THE BIGGEST SEED

The world's biggest seed is produced by the coco de mer (*Lodoicea maldivica*), a species of palm from the Seychelles Islands in the Indian Ocean.

Each seed is up to 20 inches across, can weigh up to 92 pounds and can take seven years to mature!

The name "coco de mer" (French for sea coconut) has an interesting story. French explorers found the giant seeds washed up on the coast of East Africa and islands in the Indian Ocean, and for centuries it was believed by many that the seeds were produced by a mystical coconut palm that grew at the bottom of the ocean! Eventually, coco de mer plants were discovered growing on the islands of the Seychelles, and in 1768 the myth was exploded.

OLDEST PLANT ON EARTH

Many plants can live for thousands of years, but California's bristlecone pines (*Pinus longaeva*) have the longest lives of all organisms on Earth.

The oldest bristlecone pine known to scientists grows in California's White Mountains, and is believed to be 5,068 years old. Just imagine, this same tree was alive and growing when the pyramids in Egypt were being built!

Interestingly, the bristlecone pine (as a species) has hardly changed for millions of years, as can be seen in fossils which are almost identical to the living trees.

ANCIENT WELWITSCHIA

Welwitschia mirabilis grows in the deserts of Namibia and Angola, some of the driest places on Earth. The habitat *Welwitschia* is so extreme, locals call it the "lunar landscape" (see background photo on this page).

Welwitschia is a really peculiar plant. It is related to pine trees and produces cones, although the plant itself looks nothing like a conifer. It only ever produces two adult leaves, which grow continuously (the leaves die at their tips, but grow at their bases, so always stay around the same length).

Each leaf grows by around 0.5 inches a year, and many plants have leaves with living sections of 6 feet or longer (before the end of the leaf dies and breaks apart). So the tips of these very leaves were produced up to 200 years ago, before Charles Darwin was alive!

Each *Welwitschia* plant can live for over 2,000 years (some scientists say much longer).

OLDEST BONSAI

For over 2,000 years, Japanese, Chinese, and Korean horticulturists have perfected the art of growing bonsais to produce miniature trees that mimic the shape and scale of full-grown trees. This is accomplished by continually clipping the roots and branches of the bonsai to ensure its growth is stunted, so the tree can never reach its natural size.

Particularly in Japan, some bonsais have been grown by the same family for centuries, and are passed down between the generations. Several bonsai trees are known to be over 700 years old, and a few have existed for over 1,000 years! Large bonsais need care virtually every day, so somebody must have attended to these ancient trees constantly since the year 1000. Imagine growing a potted plant and giving it to your children in the hope that in a thousand years' time, the ancestors of your children will be still growing it!

Possibly the most incredible bonsai of all is a Japanese white pine. It is 390 years old, but what makes it amazing is that it was growing in Hiroshima when the first atomic bomb was dropped in 1945. 160,000 people died in the devastating Hiroshima blast, but remarkably, it survived and is still growing today!

LARGEST SINGLE FLOWER

The plant with the largest single bloom is a corpse flower. There are many species of corpse flower, but one called *Rafflesia arnoldii* that grows in the steamy jungles of Sumatra (an island of Indonesia) produces flowers that are over 3 feet wide and can weigh over 22 pounds! The gigantic bloom lasts for only a few days before it dies and rots.

Rafflesia is a really bizarre plant. It doesn't have any leaves or roots, but grows as a parasite inside a tropical vine called *Tetrastigma*. *Rafflesia* steals all of the energy it needs to produce its gigantic flower.

Unfortunately, this specialized life cycle makes *Rafflesia* almost impossible to grow, because to grow it, you first have to grow a tropical vine, and no one has really worked out how to infect the vine with *Rafflesia*'s seeds!

three feet across

22 pounds = 10 bags of flour!

The life cycle of *Rafflesia* is fascinating. It is thought that mammals (such as shrews or wild pigs) transport the tiny seeds of *Rafflesia* and infect *Tetrastigma* vines while searching for food.

The *Rafflesia* plant then grows within the vine as a network of nutrient-absorbing threads. When it has enough energy, it erupts through the side of the vine as a brown bud.

The bud grows over many months. In some species, it may take months for the bud to reach full size. Eventually, the brown protective sheaths of the bud fall away to reveal the *Rafflesia* furled petals. Then, during a single night, the petals suddenly fold open and the massive flower is revealed, fully formed.

Little insects, such as carrion flies, are attracted by the putrid smell of the *Rafflesia* bloom and also by its color, size, and warty texture (which resembles carrion). The insects enter the flower and, while inside, they receive a dab of liquid pollen which they (inadvertently) carry to the next *Rafflesia* bloom. When fertilized, the center of the flower grows to form a cake-like structure that contains thousands of tiny seeds!

LARGEST BRANCHED FLOWER SCAPE

The record for the largest flower scape belongs to the talipot palm (*Corypha umbraculifera*) from southern India and Sri Lanka. This huge palm grows to over 75 feet tall, with a stem over 3 feet wide. It grows for up to 60 years, then produces a gigantic flower scape up to 25 feet long, which can have up to several million tiny flowers.

Amazingly, each talipot palm produces just one flower scape in its lifetime; once the fruit are ripened carrying the seeds of the next generation, the plant dies.

Like many palm species, the talipot palm is easy to grow, but due to its massive size, it is almost impossible to grow outside of gardens in the tropics!

thousands of tiny flowers

up to 30 feet high

Bromeliads are usually small, colorful plants that often grow on the branches of trees. But on rocky slopes above 9,000 feet high in the Andes Mountains of South America, there grows the world's largest species of bromeliad.

Known as *Puya raimondii*, it produces giant balls of spiky leaves up to 9 feet across on a trunk up to 15 feet tall. When it flowers, the flower scape can be 25 feet tall, so the plant may tower 48 feet or more above the ground. Each flower scape can produce up to 20,000 little white flowers!

LARGEST UNBRANCHED FLOWER SCAPE

The title of the world's largest unbranched flower scape goes to the titan arum (*Amorphophallus titanum*). This plant produces a monster bloom that can tower over 9 feet tall and over 5 feet wide.

In this species, two rings of hundreds of small flowers are positioned (a ring of male flowers above a ring of female ones). The hundreds of little flowers are grouped together inside a gigantic bell-shaped, dark red petal (called the spathe), out of which towers a huge chimney-like structure called the spadix.

This enormous flower stinks like rotting meat to attract pollinators that feed on dead animals and, during flowering, the tip of the spadix actually warms up to about human body temperature to help the stench spread into the air!

over nine feet high

five feet wide

The titan arum produces just one leaf a year, but each leaf can be the size of a small tree! The foliage produces energy, which is stored in a vast underground corm that can weigh over 730 pounds!

Each leaf stays alive for several months, then withers. The plant then produces a new leaf and the cycle is repeated, one giant leaf at a time.

Every new leaf adds more and more nutrients and starch to the underground corm until eventually the plant is ready to produce a single, spectacular bloom! The flowers last for only a few days, then die.

After flowering, berry-like fruit are produced, each containing a single seed. The seeds are dispersed by animals that eat the berries. After the berries are ripe, each giant arum plant usually becomes dormant for a few months, before beginning the production of leaves once more.

The giant arum family comprises over 200 species. They originate from tropical and subtropical parts of Asia, Africa, Australia, and nearby islands. Many produce really bizarre flowers that often have a massive spadix.

leaves the size of a small tree!

fruit

A SMELLY
RAINFOREST CHIMNEY

Many of the biggest giant arums grow in the rainforests of Borneo and Sumatra. Several species produce gigantic flowers that are more than 6 feet tall, while others produce smaller blooms borne on stems that can be 15 feet tall (for example, *Amorphophallus gigas*, shown below, with people for scale).

In these titanic blooms, the spadix works like a chimney and spreads the scent efficiently in even the faintest of jungle breezes. In some species, the spadix actually heats up to disperse the smell more effectively.

This is a major advance over other flowers that use color to attract pollinators, since insects can be attracted to the flower even if they cannot see it in the dense rainforest vegetation!

Since each giant arum plant flowers so infrequently, the nearest open bloom may be many miles away, so it is essential that the plant attracts pollinators from as far away as possible!

When they were first discovered, it was thought jungle elephants pollinated the blooms of giant arums. Botanists now know tiny carrion flies and other insects are the main pollinators!

male (above) and female (below)
flowers inside a titan arum flower

Record Holders

The titan arum family is native to Asia, Africa, and Australia. Interestingly, another group of giant aroids (called *Dracontium*) evolved in the New World and have very similar flowers to the titan arum (although not quite as large).

In North America, the eastern skunk cabbage (*Symplocarpus foetidus*) is a relative that grows in wetlands. It produces foul-smelling flowers that may be up to 6 inches tall. It is so-called because not only do the flowers stink, but also the leaves, which, when bruised, release a fragrance reminiscent of skunk!

Even though they often have terrible smells, aroids produce some of the most incredible flowers of all plants!

One of the most unusual is produced by a little-known species from Africa called *Pseudohydrosme gabunensis*.

It produces an inflorescence that resembles the funnel of a ship's horn! The flower grows up to 20 inches tall, but like most giant aroid blooms, lasts for only a few days, then dies.

It is interesting to note that, unlike most flowers, the blooms of the giant aroids often have dark interiors. This is because they mostly attract pollinators that like carrion (such as blow flies and beetles). As such, the dark color and texture mimic decaying organic matter, which the pollinators love!

WORLD'S SMELLIEST PLANTS

WHY DO SOME FLOWERS STINK?

Although most flowers produce sweet-smelling scents to attract bees and butterflies, a few have specialized to attract pollinators that like rotting meat and dung, such as carrion flies and blow flies.

In order to attract those pollinators effectively, flowers with revolting smells and unusual appearances are needed!

Some smell of rotting meat. Others stink of dung. A few smell like rancid fish! The world's smelliest flowers can be so malodorous, that you can smell some from 60 feet away or more.

Stinky
KING OF FRUIT

It's not just flowers that stink. Some fruit also use horrible smells to attract animals to eat their flesh and distribute their seeds.

One of the world's smelliest fruits is called the durian (*Durio zibethinus*). Originating in Southeast Asia, the durian looks like a spiky football. It can weigh over 10 pounds and hangs from a tree.

Inside the fruit, large seeds are covered with a yellow or cream-colored paste. The rind of the fruit and the paste have a strong odor that is often likened to rotten onions or raw sewage! People usually either hate the stink of the fruit or adore it. In many parts of Asia, this smelly fruit is regarded as a delicacy, with a taste that is savory, sweet, and creamy all at once, and it is often called the King of Fruits!

DRAGON LILY

Early in spring, the dragon lily plant (*Dracunculus vulgaris*) grows as a bud that emerges out of the ground like a dragon's snout.

After a few weeks of growing, the bud enlarges and unfurls to reveal jagged leaves that stand up to 3 feet tall and often have beautiful patterns and spots somewhat like dragon scales.

After several leaves are produced, each adult plant produces a wicked-looking flower. The flowers of the dragon lily are bewitchingly beautiful and sinister. They have a deep purple, velvety, tongue-like spathe and a large, black, horn-like spadix. As soon as the flowers open, they release a terrible stench which is described as dragon's breath! It really stinks! The smell is released on the first day of flowering, then reduces as the bloom ages. Most people describe the stink this flower creates as reminiscent of rotting meat or road kill.

Each flower may stand up to 28 inches tall and be up to 18 inches long. It opens for just a few days before it withers. The flowers are followed by green berries, which ripen to a stunning orange-red. The plant then dies down to become dormant over winter.

VOODOO LILY

The voodoo lily (*Typhonium venosum*) comes from temperate and tropical Africa and Asia, but is very cold tolerant and can even survive frost in winter.

It has a growth cycle that is similar to the dragon lily. It produces flowers that can stand up to 24 inches tall, but in this species, the flower is very narrow (usually just a few inches across).

The inside of the spathe is patterned in a really weird mix of rich maroon and yellow blotches. The outside of the spadix can be purple, brown, or green.

The spadix is often massive in proportion to the flower. It is thin, tapers to a point, and is dark red, brown, or black, like a weird, wiry alien antenna. The stench is truly revolting, and has been likened to rotting fish! Flies absolutely love the smell of the voodoo lily, and will swarm all over the flower (which is the goal of the flower's design to bring about pollination).

SMELLY FEET TREE

Some of the world's smelliest plants are totally bizarre. Believe it or not, there is a bushy shrub from Mexico that is called the Sweaty Feet Plant (*Deherainia smaragdina*). It produces small green flowers (because it attracts pollinators not by sight, but by smell), and its petals stink with a cheesy and sweaty odor!

SKUNK CABBAGE

The western skunk cabbage (*Lysichiton americanus*) is found in swamps and wet woods alongside streams in the Pacific Northwest of the United States, where it is one of the few native species in the arum family.

The plant is called skunk cabbage because of the distinctive "skunky" odor that it emits when it blooms. This odor will permeate the area where the plant grows, and can be detected even in old, dried specimens. The smell attracts its pollinators, scavenging flies and beetles.

Although similarly named and with a similar smell, the plant is easy to distinguish from the eastern skunk cabbage (see page 126).

STARFISH FLOWERS

This family of dwarf succulents includes several genera, of which *Stapelia*, *Edithcolea*, *Huernia*, and *Orbea* are the best known and most widely grown. These plants are called starfish flowers because their five-lobed blooms look like starfish. They are also sometimes called carrion flowers, because they stink of rotting meat to attract pollinators.

Starfish flower plants produce low-growing, fleshy, gray-green leafless stems that often turn bright orange or red when exposed to direct sunlight. The stems may be up to 10 inches high, are often four-sided, and are sometimes hairy. While starfish flowers might look like cacti, these stinky but spectacular plants actually belong to a completely different group of succulents.

Where Do They Come From?

Starfish flowers come from the deserts and dry plains of southern Africa, particularly Namibia, South Africa, and neighboring countries.

How Does It Grow?

In their desert habitats, starfish flowers are exposed to extreme conditions, including intense sunlight, high temperatures, and very little rain. They often grow among rocks or under other plants where they receive little protection from the searing conditions.

Their short stems creep and scramble over the ground. Many species of starfish flowers produce offshoots as they age, eventually forming clumps in areas where conditions are ideal for growth.

Starfish flower plants' thick, fleshy leaves store water very effectively, and they may survive for months without receiving any water at all! The stems tend to break into segments as the plant gets older, and the pieces fall away to root where they land, enabling the plant to spread.

While many species of starfish flower produce blooms that are 2-3 inches across, the biggest of all (*Stapelia gigantea*) produces flowers that can be up to 16 inches in diameter!

The blooms of starfish flowers are five-lobed, flat, and often have dramatic and intricate banded or spotted patterns of red, purple, yellow, orange, and black. The delicate reproductive parts are in the middle of the flower, often arranged in a star shape.

The striking colors and patterns make the flowers contrast with the otherwise uniform desert landscape, so they stand out to attract pollinators.

Amazingly, the flowers of many starfish flowers have intricate patterns visible only in ultraviolet light, which we humans cannot see. However, these secret patterns make the flowers even more eye-catching in the UV-sensitive vision of pollinating insects!

The flowers also mimic the body of a dead animal. Many species have petals that are covered in hairs with uneven surfaces to mimic decaying animal matter. Some starfish flowers have a hole in the center of the bloom to resemble a natural opening or wound. In some species, each flower may open for only a few days; in others, the blooms may last for a week or more.

The deception is very effective. Flies are fooled into laying their eggs on the flowers, thinking the petals are rotting meat. While they look for the best place to lay their eggs, they inadvertently pollinate the blooms. Often, the fly eggs hatch out into tiny maggots that quickly die of starvation.

What Does It Smell Like?

Starfish flowers really stink!

In many species, the smell is a putrid odor of rotting carrion that attracts blow flies. Sometimes people describe the stench as resembling rancid fish, rotting meat, or even poo! Flowers are usually particularly smelly on hot afternoons, and the scent can be carried for many feet.

If you want to surprise your parents or neighbors with a really terrible smell, this is the perfect plant to grow!

Many starfish flowers are really easy to grow and are extremely low maintenance. The species *Stapelia variegata* is one of the easiest. It has really interesting flowers and is recommended for the beginner. Treat it like a cactus with plenty of sun and warm conditions year round. Plant it in sandy, well-drained soil and water just once a week during the summer.

CARNIVOROUS PLANTS

Over 800 species of plants eat insects and other small animals. They are called carnivorous plants, and include some of the most unusual and highly specialized of all plant species.

To be carnivorous, a plant must be able to attract, trap, kill, and digest prey and then absorb the nutrients that are released.

Eating animals enables carnivorous plants to obtain nutrients that they need to grow. This allows carnivorous plants to grow in areas where many non-carnivorous plants can't survive.

As such, most carnivorous plants grow in nutrient-poor habitats such as swampy wetlands, and some even grow on bare rock!

The traps of carnivorous plants are not flowers but highly evolved leaves that are modified to capture prey. They are often very colorful, and so function a little like petals.

BIGGEST ANIMAL PREY

Most carnivorous plants catch insects and other invertebrates, but several of the biggest species of pitcher plants (such as *Nepenthes rajah*) are known occasionally to trap shrews, mice, and even rats!

Really large sundews (such as *Drosera binata*) can catch birds, and even the Venus's flytrap can trap small frogs and baby lizards!

The capture of vertebrates by carnivorous plants is more accidental than by design. But still impressive!

prey

LIFE AND DEATH

Although the leaves of carnivorous plants evolved to kill animals, sometimes they are also lifelines!

Many species or organisms have evolved partnerships and symbiotic relationships with carnivorous plants.

The tropical pitcher plants (*Nepenthes*) can have entire ecosystems of life that live with the plants' deadly traps, sometimes with dozens of species!

Capsid bugs have learned to live on the sticky leaves of sundews and often steal prey! These commensal organisms (known as "infauna") have to be very careful. If they make a mistake, they may become the plant's next meal.

NATURAL COOKING POTS

Believe it or not, in many areas across Southeast Asia, the traps of tropical pitcher plants are used in cooking!

In Malaysia, Indonesia, Thailand, Cambodia, and elsewhere, the pitchers are stuffed with rice and steamed to make delicious snacks!

As the pitchers catch insect prey, it is important to wash out old traps before adding the rice; otherwise, you end up with the dead bugs mixed in with the rice! Pitchers are still used in this way today and often sold in local markets!

One of the most popular species used for cooking is *Nepenthes ampullaria* (pictured here). Would you eat rice cooked in a pitcher plant?

VENUS'S FLYTRAP

The world's most famous carnivorous plant is the Venus's flytrap (*Dionaea muscipula*). This plant is unmistakable, with its dramatic-looking toothed leaves and high-speed snap-trap action.

The trapping process is really remarkable. The trap consists of two hinged lobes. Each lobe has three trigger hairs. The lobes are usually very colorful and secrete drops of nectar as a form of bait.

Prey (usually insects) are attracted and land on the lobes. If contact is made twice with trigger hairs, the trap snaps shut in a fraction of a second. The toothed edges interlock, and slowly the lobes squeeze together, forming a seal. The space inside then fills with digestive juices that rapidly break down prey!

The trap does not close if the trigger hairs are touched just once. This is to keep raindrops from accidentally setting off the trap and wasting energy!

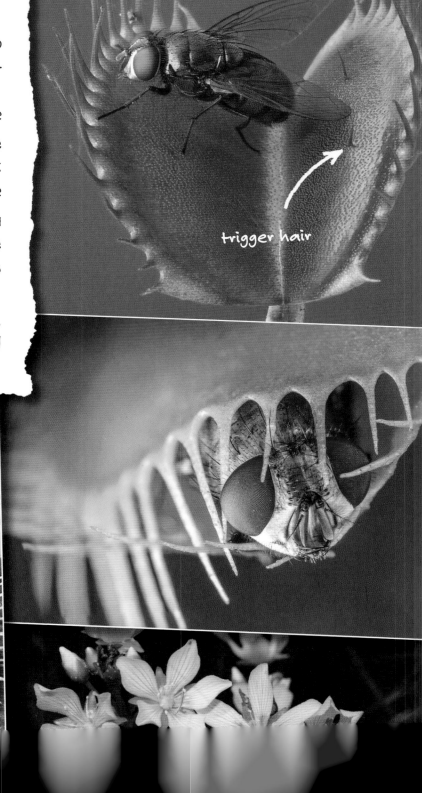

trigger hair

trap

WATERWHEEL PLANT

The *Venus's flytrap* has an aquatic relative that is just as amazing!

The waterwheel plant (*Aldrovanda vesiculosa*) produces underwater "snap traps" that are up to 0.3 inches across.

They work in exactly the same way as the traps of the *Venus's flytrap*, but in some ways are even more remarkable as they close even more quickly (despite the water resistance).

The waterwheel plant's traps have been recorded to snap shut in 0.01 to 0.02 seconds! They mostly capture mosquito larvae and other tiny aquatic invertebrates, but they also can trap vertebrates, including tadpoles and fish fry!

Although they look very different, the *Venus's flytrap* and the waterwheel plant are related, and both evolved from sticky-leaved carnivorous plants.

prey

FLYPAPER TRAPS

There are many genera of sticky-leaved carnivorous plants that trap insects like flypaper! The plants produce colorful leaves lined with droplets of sticky glue. When insects land on the leaves, they become stuck and eventually suffocate and die.

The two most widespread groups of flypaper traps are the sundews (*Drosera*) and butterworts (*Pinguicula*).

Though not as fast-moving as the Venus's flytrap, the leaves and tentacles of most sundews and many butterworts can move. In some species, a leaf will fold over the struggling victim in a matter of minutes! Additionally, a few pygmy sundews have specialized "snap tentacles", which move extremely quickly and flick prey into the middle of the leaf!

Once prey is caught, the plants release enzymes and digestive fluids that pool onto the leaf and break the victim's body down. The foliage has glands on its surface that absorb the resultant soup of nutrients!

Most flypaper traps are quite small, although the very biggest produce leaves 20 inches long. One genus (*Roridula*) has resin-based glue that is so powerful that small birds are known to have been caught by it!

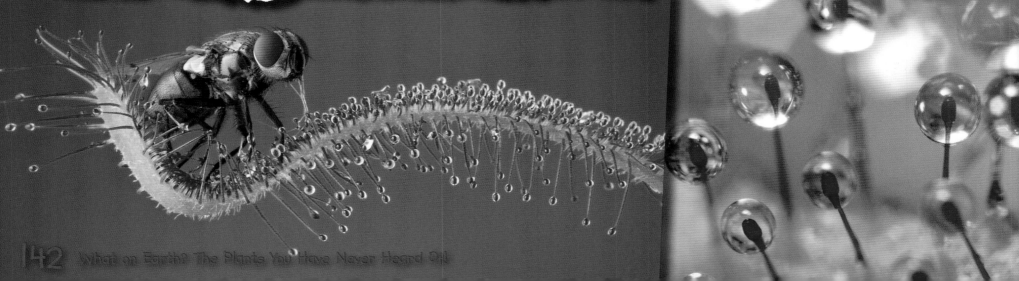

prey

PITCHER PLANTS

Pitcher plants are the largest and most spectacular of all carnivorous plants. There are seven genera that occur across the world, the biggest being the tropical pitcher plants (*Nepenthes*) and the trumpet pitcher plants (*Sarracenia*).

All pitcher plants catch prey in essentially the same way.

They produce leaves that form vessels (called "pitchers") that contain rainwater and other fluids. The pitchers are usually very colorful and often have lots of nectar glands, creating a sweet scent like a flower.

Insects are attracted to the trap and try to reach the nectar (which is usually positioned above the pitcher opening). The surface of the pitcher near the nectar is ultra-slippery and often covered with wax.

As the insect scales the pitcher to reach the nectar bait, it puts itself in a dangerous position. One slip and it falls straight into the trap, landing in digestive liquid within. The inner surface of the pitcher is slippery and prevents the victim from escaping, and it eventually drowns or suffocates.

Most species of pitcher plants produce enzymes which digest the body of the prey so that the plant can then absorb the nutrients.

prey attracted to bait

COBRA LILIES

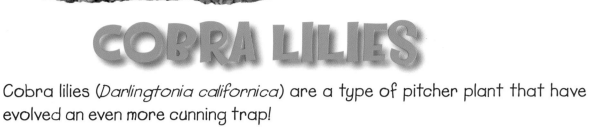

Cobra lilies (*Darlingtonia californica*) are a type of pitcher plant that have evolved an even more cunning trap!

They produce leaves that are shaped just like striking cobras! The head of the cobra is lined with lots of transparent windows.

Insects are attracted to nectar that is secreted from glands on a moustache-like appendage. At the top of the appendage, there is a large entrance hole.

Light shines through the transparent windows and illuminates the interior of the trap. After they have had their fill of nectar, the insects fly up through the entrance hole (thinking the bright light above is the sky).

But once inside, the curvature of the trap bounces the prey down the tubular pitcher, where downward-pointing hairs and the slippery interior surfaces prevent the prey from escaping.

TOILET BOWLS

Believe it or not, a few species of pitcher plants (such as *Nepenthes lowii*, above) produce pitchers with upright lids that allow small mammals like tree shrews (see insert above) to feed from them.

These animals rarely end up as food, but regularly poop while drinking from the pitchers. Anything they produce falls straight into the pitcher below, providing the plants with nutrients!

BLADDERWORTS

Bladderworts (*Utricularia*) are the most innocent-looking of all carnivorous plants ... but their beauty hides a deadly secret.

They grow in wetlands, ponds, or even as epiphytes (growing on the branches of trees). They produce colorful flowers and small leaves, but also grow hundreds of tiny "bladder traps" that are specialized for catching tiny prey in the soil or underwater.

The bladder traps are white, oval capsules that are just 0.1-0.5 inches across. They inspire the plant's English name.

On the inside of the bladders, there are special glands that pump out all air and water, causing the bladder to have low internal pressure.

At one end of the bladder, there is a little trapdoor next to a series of sensitive trigger hairs.

When a tiny creature (such as a mosquito larva) moves past the trap and touches a trigger hair, the trapdoor springs open.

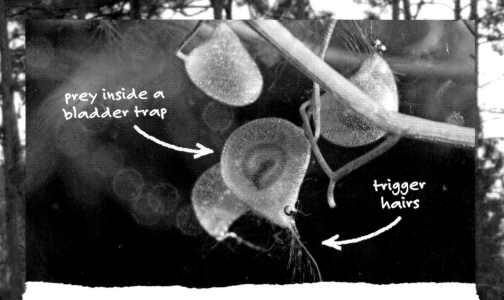

prey inside a bladder trap

trigger hairs

The tiny animal eventually suffocates inside the bladder, and the little trap is flooded with enzymes. The prey is quickly digested, and the plant absorbs the resulting nutrients!

The trap then resets and is ready to capture more prey! Each plant may have thousands of bladders.

Due to the low internal pressure inside the bladder, as the trap door opens, the prey is immediately sucked inside. The little trapdoor then quickly shuts, imprisoning the victim inside the bladder!

The trapping process takes place within a fraction of a second, and the prey is captured before it has any chance of escape.

Rainbow Flowers

Bladderworts have beautiful flowers that come in every color of the rainbow.

The blooms of most species are tiny (less than 0.5 inches across), although a few species from South America produce really showy blooms that may be over 2 inches wide! The majority of species have flowers that are yellow, purple, or white.

THE LOST WORLD

Carnivorous plants occur across the world, on every continent except Antarctica. Overall, carnivory is very rare in the plant kingdom (with less than 0.01% of all plant species being carnivorous).

Most carnivorous plants live in wetland areas where the soil is leached and devoid of nutrients. In such habitats, carnivorous plants have a real advantage over non-carnivorous plants and can even become the dominant vegetation.

The spectacular tepui mountains of Venezuela rise up to 3,000 feet over the surrounding rainforest. These massive sandstone plateaus are among the wettest places on Earth. Nutrients are continually washed over their sides. Their summits are home to the greatest concentrations of carnivorous plants in the world, in some cases with dozens of species growing together!

What on Earth? The Plants You Have Never Heard Of!

FASCINATING FUNGI

Fungi are not plants. They belong to a completely different grouping of organisms. However, they do bear many parallels to plants, and lots of plant species have extremely close partnerships with fungi. Some plants cannot live without fungi, such as many orchids and lichen-algae.

Around 150,000 species of fungi have been described to date, although thousands more await classification and naming. Fungi have complex life cycles that begin with spores. The spores germinate and form a mycelium (an interconnected network of hyphae) and eventually a fruit body (such as a mushroom).

Many fungi are extremely toxic (some can even be deadly). <u>Never</u> eat wild mushrooms unless identified by an expert. Over the following pages, a few fascinating species of fungi are profiled.

PLANT-FUNGI PARTNERS

Lichens are composite organisms that arise from algae or cyanobacteria living among filaments of fungi. In some cases, the algae and fungi cannot survive unless they grow together as lichens. Together, they form flat or leaf-like structures that grow for decades or more.

fruit bodies

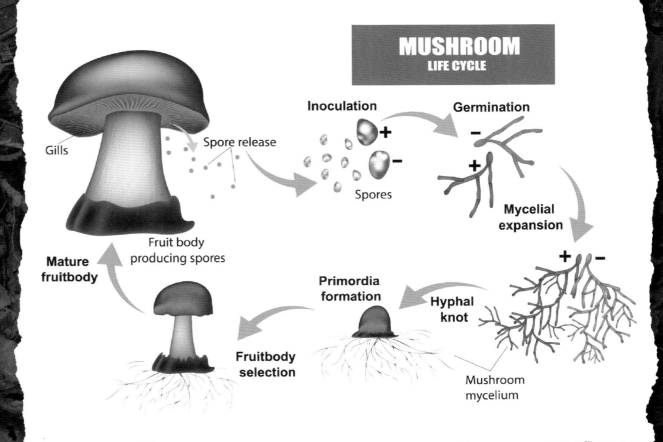

MUSHROOM
LIFE CYCLE

Gills

Spore release

Mature fruitbody

Fruit body producing spores

Spores

Inoculation

Germination

+

−

−

+

Mycelial expansion

+

−

Fruitbody selection

Primordia formation

Hyphal knot

Mushroom mycelium

BLEEDING TOOTH FUNGUS

The bleeding tooth fungus (*Hydnellum peckii*) produces fruit bodies that grow into a funnel shape. They are usually white, although they can be highly variable. Young, moist fruit bodies "bleed" bright red droplets of thick liquid. This gooey "blood" is actually a type of sap that is created by a process called guttation. When the soil surrounding the fungus becomes very wet, it may force water into the fungus through the process of osmosis. This creates pressure and pushes fluid out of the top of the fruit bodies, creating the eerie droplets!

BIRD'S NEST FUNGI

Bird's nest fungi are a group (called the *Nidulariaceae*) which produce fruit bodies that resemble tiny birds' nests filled with eggs! The "eggs" are specialized structures called peridioles and contain the spores. The "nests" act as splash-cups. When a raindrop hits one at a certain angle, the walls are shaped so that the eggs are expelled up to 3 feet away from the cup. Some species have a sticky trailing thread (called a funicular cord) that remains attached to the peridiole. The spores are thought to be ingested by herbivores and grow in their droppings to continue the life cycle.

WITCH'S CAULDRON FUNGUS

The witch's cauldron fungus (*Sarcosoma globosum*) is found along streams and brooks in northern Europe and North America. It produces fruit bodies that may be up to 4 inches in diameter, brown or black in color, and filled with black goo (just like a potion in a witch's cauldron!). Mycologists (fungi experts) do not know what the purpose of the black goo is. Some have suggested that it serves as a form of bait for animal visitors that transport spores and aid the distribution of the fungus.

PUFFBALLS

Puffballs are a diverse group of fungi that produce large, round, spongy fruit bodies that release clouds of brown dust-like spores when impacted. The largest puffballs may grow to more than 16 inches across and may produce literally billions of spores. If every spore germinated and grew to full size, in three generations puffballs would have the mass of the Earth!

VEIL FUNGI

Many species of fungi produce incredibly elaborate fruit bodies, often with striking lacy "skirts", for example the long net stinkhorn (*Phallus indusiatus*, shown to the right) and the yellow bridal veil fungi (*Phallus multicolor*). In these species, the fruit bodies grow up to 10 inches tall with a conical bell-shaped cap that is covered with greenish-brown spore-containing slime. Flies and other insects eat the slime and disperse the spores. The lacy "skirt" hangs from beneath the cap and nearly reaches the ground. It may aid scent dispersal and may make the fungus conspicuous to aid spore distribution.

EARTHSTARS

Earthstars are a group of around 65 species of fungi that are related to puffballs. They produce distinctive fruit bodies which split open (often triggered by wet weather). The segments of the fruit body curl backward forming a star shape, and raise a spherical spore sac upward. Large drops of rain that fall onto the spore sac cause it to puff out clouds of spores or spray droplets of spore-rich fluid. The spores are carried in the wind or washed to new habitat. In most species of earthstars, the fruit bodies are 2-4 inches wide and white, cream, or brown in color.

GLOWING FUNGI

Worldwide, at least 80 species of fungi are known to glow, and in all cases they produce greenish light.

Still to this day, scientists do not know why these fungi glow. Some believe it is a by-product of the fungi breaking down organic matter. Others hold that the glow attracts animals that could help in dispersing the fungi spores.

Among the most common glowing fungi are small round green pepe (*Mycena chlorophos*) and the larger ghost mushroom (*Omphalotus nidiformis*). Both of these species are shown here.

PHOTOGRAPHIC CREDITS

The publisher and author would like to thank all those photographers and image makers who have contributed to this book. SS = Shutterstock.

Front Cover: Aphelleon/SS, Cathy Keifer/SS, Mike Clifford, Anna ART/SS, D. Kucharski K. Kucharska/SS; **1:** Aom Khuanphirom/SS, Don Mammoser/SS, Dancestrokes/SS, Zvone/SS, Sanit Fuangnakhon/SS, Khuroshvili Ilya/SS; **2:** Artlusy/SS, Business stock/SS, Khuroshvili Ilya/SS; **3:** Khuroshvili Ilya/SS, Stewart McPherson; **4:** areeya_ann/SS, 285349541/SS, Oleksandra Klestova/SS; **5:** Oleksandra Klestova/SS; **6:** Aphelleon/SS; **7:** Chansom Pantip/SS, Dirk Ercken/SS, Sanit Fuangnakhon/SS, Anton Kozyrev/SS, Taweesak Sriwannawit/SS; **8:** Daniel Eskridge/SS, Orla/SS, Oleksandra Klestova/SS; **9:** GUDKOV ANDREY/SS; **10:** Simia Attentive/SS, udaix/SS, alinabel/SS, Oleksandra Klestova/SS; **11:** Jezper/SS, K_E_N/SS, Ethan Daniels/SS, Ammak/SS, KYTan/SS, yakonstant/SS, Thomas Retterath/SS; **12:** EAKARAT BUANOI/SS, Chansom Pantip/SS, VectorMine/SS, Oleksandra Klestova/SS; **13:** Aom Khuanphirom/SS, Business stock/SS, Oleksandra Klestova/SS, COLOA Studio/SS, Milena Lachowicz/SS, Elif Bayraktar/SS, Leriaphoto/SS, Alex K.L. Fleming/SS, BlueSnap/SS, Simon Groewe/SS, APCat/SS, Nine Johnson/SS, Trek Bears Photography/SS; **14:** VectorMine/SS; **15:** Artlusy/SS, VectorMine/SS, Quality Stock Arts/SS, LDarin/SS, Sanit Fuangnakhon/SS, studio2013/SS; **16:** udaix/SS, Oleksandra Klestova/SS; Chansom Pantip/SS; **17:** Oleksandra Klestova/SS, udaix/SS, VectorMine/SS, Chansom Pantip/SS; **18:** Dirk Ercken/SS, VectorMine/SS, desdemona72/SS, Oleksandra Klestova/SS; **19:** Jane Rix/SS, Vadim Nefedoff/SS, PatrickLauzon photographe/SS, Oleksandra Klestova/SS; **20:** RethaAretha/SS, Mark Baldwin/SS, Ondrej Prosicky/SS, Anton Petrus/SS, Oleksandra Klestova/SS; **21:** Sergey Novikov/SS, neenawat khenyothaa/SS, Simon Dannhauer/SS, Arnain/SS, Oleksandra Klestova/SS; **22:** Damsea/SS, Gianfranco Vivi/SS, KGrif/SS, Valerii_M/SS, Oleksandra Klestova/SS; **23:** Jasper Suijten/SS, Oliver Osvald/SS, Irina Mos/SS, khwanchai/SS, Oleksandra Klestova/SS; **24:** BorneoRimbawan/SS, mbarredo/SS; **25:** BorneoRimbawan/SS, VectorMine/SS, Sorn340 Studio Images/SS, John Bill/SS, Dinael Oropeza/SS, Hugh Lansdown/SS; **26:** KUMA-MON/SS, noicherrybeans/SS, bamboovn/SS, MajestiX B/SS, BudiWin/SS, Nick Greaves/SS, Fabrizio Guarisco/SS, Martin Leber/SS; **27:** Flower_Garden/SS, Grisha Bruev/SS, Media Marketing/SS; **28:** Viktor Loki/SS, Stephen Fretwell, Viktor Loki/SS, cotosa/SS, 100Y Design/SS; **29:** Mark Heighes/SS, Beatrice Sirinuntananon/SS, Yukiakari/SS, songsak/SS, Mark Heighes/SS, www.strangewonderfulthings.com, Bos11/SS, New Line/SS, 100Y Design/SS; **30:** Wildnerdpix/SS, Jody./SS, l & bl www.flickr.com/photos/laajala/, r Wathana/SS; **31:** Francisco Herrera/SS, Avery Chan; **32:** Shulevskyy Volodymyr/SS; **33:** ittisak boonphardpai/SS, INTERTOURIST/SS, S-JO/SS, Shulevskyy Volodymyr/SS, 1348091423/SS, Kazakov Maksim/SS; **34:** Pimonpim T/SS, Alex Staroseltsev/SS, noicherrybeans/SS, Soulikone Thongsamouth/SS, Anna ART/SS; **35:** Massimiliano Finzi/SS, Gardens by Design/SS, Manfred Ruckszio/SS, Don Mammoser/SS, NECHAPHAT/SS, p_nam/SS, NeCoTi/SS, Chansom Pantip/SS; **36:** Han-Lin/SS, Nublee bin Shamsu Bahar/SS; **37:** guentermanaus/SS; **38:** Djohan Shahrin/SS; **39:** Djohan Shahrin/SS, Bonma Suriya/SS; **40:** Kelly Richter/SS; **41:** Raphael Comber Sales/SS, Bruno Martins Imagens/SS; **42:** Nopparat Promtha/SS, Jukov studio/SS, lovelyday12/SS, Darika Nachiangmai/SS, Pushkarenko Mariya/SS, Colorshadow/SS, AlessandroZocc/SS, Bashutskyy/SS, sergei kochetov/SS, Peter Hermes, nadia_if/SS, Furian/SS; **43:** nadia_if/SS, cinema99/SS, Elsa van Dyk/SS,

Pungky Nanda PratamaSS, Suchat tepruang/SS, Heartkiki/SS; **44:** MariLila/SS, Cynthia Liang/SS, S-F/SS, Serenethos/SS, Anna Kucherova/SS, FPWing/SS; **45:** Cynthia Liang/SS, S-F/SS, Stephen Smith, margouillat photo/SS; **46:** Lebedeva Olga/SS, Neale Cousland/SS, lineartestpilot/SS, LENA GABRILOVICH/SS, naramit/SS; **47:** Lebedeva Olga/SS, Ramon L. Farinos/SS, picturepartners/SS, CC BY-SA 4.0/Didier Descouens, ThomasLENNE/SS, Halfmine.mamie/SS, Neale Couslan/SS, Ramon L. Farinos/SS, Picture Partners/SS; **48:** photogal/SS, CG__Photography/SS, Natalia Korshunova/SS, ArtCookStudio/SS, Izlan Somai/SS, Alex Coan/SS, Michaelpuche/SS; **49:** David Pimborough/SS, Irina Solatges/SS; **50:** 5PH/SS, vaivirga/SS, Anastasia_Panait/SS, Rosemarie Mosteller/SS; **51:** Teri Virbickis/SS, Dani Vincek/SS, Natasha Breen/SS, VectoryFloor/SS; **52:** NBArt_Ryujin/SS, Boonchuay1970/SS, SOMCHAI DISSALUNG/SS; **53:** DMHai/SS, Maria Uspenskaya/SS, Deenida/SS; **54:** nikiteev_konstantin /SS, nutua/SS, CC2 Laughlin Elkin; **55:** box t & b fruitmould.com, Rashevskyi Viacheslav/SS, Sebastian Kaulitzki/SS, fruitmould.com; **56:** Anjo Kan/SS, Radoslav Kellner/SS; **57:** MaxAsrory/SS, Alex Stemmers/SS, ilen nalishawa/SS, jiangdi/SS, SnowWhiteimages/SS, Madlen/SS; **58:** Triff/SS, NABODIN/SS, Rattiya Thongdumhyu/SS, Firn/SS, VectorMine/SS, Barbol/SS; **59:** Chansom Pantip/SS, sarawut muensang/SS, Rybnikova Olga/SS, Chursina Viktoriia/SS, Kaotunshutter/SS, Stewart McPherson, patchii/SS; **60:** komkrit Preechachanwate/SS, Sapsiwai/SS, irin-k/SS; **61:** Gardens by Design/SS, David_Maddock/SS, Peter Kunasz/SS; **62:** Stewart McPherson; **63:** Stewart McPherson; **64:** Mike Clifford; **65:** JoziJozi Photography/SS, pisces2386/SS, photo of green crowned brilliant by Hans Hillewaert/wikipedia CC BY-SA 3.0; **66:** AjayTvm/SS, shutting/SS; **67:** GlanceDays/SS; **68:** Krzysztof Ziarnek, Kenraiz/Wikipedia - CC BY-SA 4.0; **69:** Sethu Krishna/SS, Syamili R V/SS, wasanajai/SS; **70:** Alexey_Ivanov/SS, kristof lauwers/SS, leopictures/SS, Flower_Garden/SS; **71:** mizy/SS, Morphart Creation/SS, Paco Moreno/SS, Akif CUBUK/SS; **72:** Stewart McPherson; **73:** JIANG TIANMU/SS, Peter Bowman/SS; **74:** Mark Green/SS, Charles HB Mercer/SS, tony mills/SS, asharkyu/SS, EQRoy/SS, vitormarigo/SS; **75:** dinodentist/SS, alphashooter/SS, JIPEN/SS, SARIN KUNTHONG/SS, Thanisnan Sukprasert/SS, Annabel Cordova/SS, Chansom Pantip/SS; **76:** mspoli/SS, Khun Ta/SS; **77:** Kaotunshutter/SS, Oldboys/SS, Chun photographer/SS, Baramyou0708/SS, Pintip Kasemsarn/SS; **78:** pramot/SS, Kaotunshutter/SS, IvanaStevanoski/SS, Kaotunshutter/SS, kamnuan/SS, COULANGES/SS; **79:** IrinaK/SS, PhotoAdventure Studio/SS, patchii/SS; **80:** Gabor Kovacs Photography/SS, Piboon Suwankosai/SS; **81:** kojihirano/SS, Brenda Brooks/SS, Nate Hovee/SS, Natalia van D/SS, ubonwanu/SS; **82:** krolya25, azure1, Markus_272, Chrispo, Incomible/SS; **83:** Toca Marine/SS, Danita Delimont/SS; **84:** azure1/SS, FILOSOFIA/SS, Victoria Tucholka/SS, Alex Farias/SS, zedspider/SS, DNikolaev/SS; **85:** Simon Dannhauer/SS, Rasmus Holmboe Dahl/SS, Angel DiBilio/SS, Sea_Monkey/SS, Angel DiBilio/SS; **86:** Urban Reiver/SS, AS Inc/SS, Eivaisla/SS, Marlon Lopez MMG1 Design/SS, Paul Latham/SS; **87:** svetlanabalyn/SS, sirastock/SS, hifashion/SS, Ksenia Ragozina/SS, Lyudmila Lucienne/SS; **88:** Massimiliano Finzi/SS, Kagai19927/SS, Pavaphon Supanantananont/SS, Akif CUBUK/SS, guentermanaus/SS, Eldred Lim/SS, Naoki Takebayashi/Wikipedia - CC BY-SA 4.0, Chansom Pantip/SS; **89:** lr.s/SS, Kletr/SS, Pierre-Yves Babelon/SS, IamTK/SS, portumen/SS; **90:** Michail_Vorobyev/SS, Valentyna Chukhlyebova/SS, JurateBuiviene/SS; **91:** Vectorpocket/SS, Doug J Moore/SS; **92:** Bruce Rolff/SS, David Herraez Calzada/SS, Photo Win1/SS, Foto-Ruhrgebiet/SS, LianeM/SS, Peter Turner Photography/SS, danielo/SS; **93:**

THE AUTHOR

Stewart McPherson is a British naturalist, author, and filmmaker. He spent 10 years climbing 300 mountains across the world to study and photograph carnivorous plants to write a series of 30 books. Along the way, he co-discovered and co-named 35 new species/varieties, including some of the largest carnivorous pitcher plants ever discovered.

Between 2012 and 2015, Stewart and a camera team traveled to all of the UK Overseas Territories to film the *Britain's Treasure Islands* documentary series for BBC and SBS. The accompanying book was distributed widely, and sponsored copies were donated to 5,350 schools and 2,000 libraries.

In 2019, Stewart worked closely with the Don Hanson Charitable Foundation to create and donate boxes of educational resources to 10,000 schools across the UK to inspire students' learning and passion for conservation.

In 2020, he worked with the Jane Goodall Institute Australia and the Don Hanson Charitable Foundation to send boxes of resources to 4,000 Australian schools and 20,000 schools across the UK. He worked with the same organizations in 2021 to send further resource boxes to 4,000 Australian schools and 8,000 schools across the UK.

www.stewartmcpherson.com

INDEX